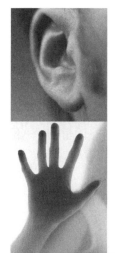

P9-DGU-150

Learning
Style
Perspectives

IMPACT IN THE CLASSROOM

Lynne
Celli
Sarasin

Learning Style Perspectives: Impact in the Classroom
by Lynne Celli Sarasin

Copyright © 2006

2nd Edition

Atwood Publishing
Madison, WI
www.atwoodpublishing.com

All rights reserved.
Printed in the United States of America

Cover and text design © TLC Graphics, www.TLCGraphics.com

ISBN: 978-1-8918595-1-9

Library of Congress Cataloging-in-Publication Data

Sarasin, Lynne Celli.
   Learning style perspectives : impact in the classroom / by Lynne Celli
Sarasin.– 2nd ed.
      p. cm.
   Includes bibliographical references and index.
   ISBN-13: 978-1-891859-51-9
   1. Learning. 2. Cognitive styles. 3. College students–Psychology.
I. Title.

   LB1060.S27 2006
   370.15'23–dc22
                              2006004704

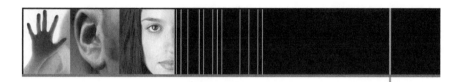

Dedication

To my family and friends, a sincere thank you for the support you have given me throughout the "awesome adventure" of completing this project. Your love and friendship are treasures in my life.

Especially to my children, Melissa, Billy, and Jamie, you have been the lights of my life. You, too, have always been true supports to me in everything that I have done, personally and professionally. I will forever be grateful for the joy you have brought me and the love you share with me every day.

Always remember: anything that you dream you can accomplish and you should dream great dreams. As you learn throughout your lifetimes, acquire as much knowledge as possible, be honest, hope for the future, and keep love in your hearts and you will accomplish much.

I love you with all my heart!

Mom

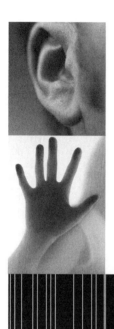

Table of Contents

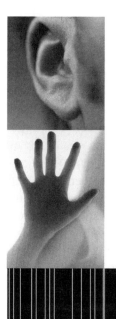

Preface

When instructors begin to think about their students and about their student's learning success, they cannot help but acknowledge the importance of individual learning styles as a significant contributor to overall learning success. It is critical for instructors to first become familiar with learning styles research, then sift through the myriad of approaches to understanding learning styles and the variety of labels surrounding learning styles, and finally apply the research to concrete learning situations.

Instructors at the postsecondary level have a certain responsibility for understanding and applying learning styles research because teaching strategies at this level have traditionally been centered around the lecture. Therefore, students with learning styles that are not compatible with the traditional lecture approach will be at a disadvantage in a learning situation such as this and may not succeed unless their instructors can accommodate their styles. Current research points to the fact that postsecondary instructors still are having difficulty incorporating learning styles research into their delivery of information. PK-12 teachers have a wealth of professional development and instruction in this area, greatly due to the new standards movement. As Sagor (2003) states, it is critical to have students succeed in a wide variety of settings, not just as a result of the lecture mode. Some departments, such as Business Management, that lend themselves to more diverse presentations often require students to work in groups to present a group research project on a particular topic. This format encourages learning in a much different way than the mere lecture. Some larger institutions of higher education that have large sections of students in courses, 150–250 students each, now require that students meet additional time during a regular week in smaller groups. During this smaller group meeting time, students have the opportunity to interact with the instructor and other students personally. This smaller type of format may assist students with diverse learning styles in understanding information and course material, as they interact with course material and each other.

In discussions and interviews with faculty there is still the common issue with time management and the appropriate instruction of the information and data necessary to be covered during a semester. Many faculty have at least discussed the issue of planning in diverse ways, such as looking at a unit's worth of work or a week's worth of work, and varying presentation methods from day to day. This ensures that some students will not feel completely ill at ease consistently as they proceed through a full semester's worth of work in any given course.

In Chapter 2, the Tour of Learning Styles chapter, the Bernice McCarthy 4MAT System will be used as an example of diversifying teaching strategies. Sagor (2003) believes that having a single lesson or various lessons in a unit with presentation styles that rotate around the 4MAT wheel will ensure a variety for all learners.

Diversifying teaching strategies to meet the learning needs of all learners requires that teachers update their planning. Also in discussions and interviews, faculty have indicated that this can be done when normal preparations for implementation of lessons take place. These normal lesson preparations are assumed to take place on a regular basis. Professional faculty prepare each class for each new semester individually. Taking the time to not only review updated research on topics being taught, but to plan implementation strategies that are varied will promote short and long term student academic success. After all, the goal of education at any level is to arm students with skills and strategies that will prepare them for a multitude of life situations and circumstances.

The purpose of this book is to acquaint the reader with learning styles research, the variety of labels used, and teaching strategies that can help all students learn. It is a practical attempt to organize the research into an applicable perspective, to provide instructors with concrete examples of how to apply the learning styles research to classroom situations.

The goal of this book is to give instructors a primer on learning styles. This book synthesizes contemporary learning styles research into a system that is easily transferable to the postsecondary classroom, designating students in terms of auditory, visual, and tactile strengths, then suggesting teaching strategies that address these three learning styles.

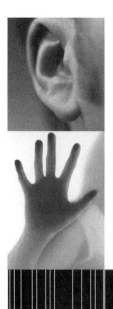

The Significance of Learning Styles

CHAPTER ONE

C urrent research in education suggests that teachers need to become aware that each of their students is unique. A very important aspect of the differences among students is learning styles.

The concept of learning style has been defined as a certain specified pattern of behavior and/or performance according to which the individual approaches a learning experience, a way in which the individual takes in new information and develops new skills, and the process by which the individual retains new information or new skills. Understanding learning styles includes understanding behaviors when approaching a learning experience, when involved in a learning experience, when evaluating a learning experience, and when applying new information and skills to situations in life.

1

Sheal (1989) believes that one of the most important responsibilities of instructors today is to find out what is happening in the minds of their students. It is through attempting to figure out what is in those minds and exactly how students are thinking that instructors begin to understand the importance of knowing about learning styles and how they relate to the success of their students. They then can consider how to transfer information from research about learning styles into what they do in the classroom.

Because of the complexity of the learning processes and because of growing research in this area, all teachers should keep current on methodologies and strategies. Unfortunately, instructors at the postsecondary level are generally specialists in their fields but have little experience with pedagogical and andragogical research. It is critical that postsecondary instructors, whatever their field and setting, appreciate the complexity of the learning process and understand about learning styles and how they relate to learning success.

Importance of Understanding Learning Styles

Evidence suggests that the interaction among teaching styles and learning styles and the classroom environment is primary to the structure and process of learning (Anderson 1995). Research indicates that the relationship between learning styles and teaching styles is a factor in the success of postsecondary students.

The differences among learning styles have become more striking as our learning communities in higher education have become more diverse. Traditionally, the educational system has favored certain types of learners; they succeeded and went on to higher education, while other types of learners generally did not. But as higher education becomes more accessible, our students are more representative of the general population, which means a greater diversity in learning styles.

To teach more effectively, instructors need to know more about differences in learning and better appreciate the variety of learning styles. To put it simply, they need to be better able to answer the question, How do my students perceive and process information?

Instructors who know about learning styles and appreciate the differences among their students should be willing to change their teaching strategies and techniques. They should try to ensure that their methods, materials, and resources fit the ways in which their students learn and maximize the learning potential of each student.

To accommodate these different styles and work more effectively with each student, our approach to education should be holistic or global. A holistic approach to strategies, lessons, and activities will more likely allow us to better address the learning needs and strengths of our students.

O'Neil (1990) notes that teaching in terms of individual learning styles emphasizes the positive: understanding a student's learning style puts the focus on that student's strengths, rather than on his or her weaknesses.

Felder (1996) states that if a mismatch is present between the teacher's teaching style and the students' learning styles, students tend to become bored and may even become inattentive. These negative responses in a classroom setting do not produce positive academic achievement. Rather, they produce a setting whereby teachers do not know what their students are truly capable of achieving. It is important for teachers to become aware of learning styles in advance of the negative effects surfacing. If teachers identify various learning styles and plan lessons and activities that are varied in nature, this will encourage students to be motivated and feel that they really can master the new material and become successful using this new material. It is critical for teachers to be sure that if they do have negative effects that surface, that they look to themselves first before they automatically look to the students. Only after a substantive effort to vary presentation of new material can one say that individual learning styles have been addressed through multifaceted teaching.

As we take this more positive approach toward our students, we should make their learning environment more positive. Students must feel free to take risks without fear of negative consequences. Students who feel safe are more likely to open up to new experiences, information, concepts, and activities.

To accommodate diverse learning styles in an environment in which students feel comfortable taking risks is simply to treat all students fairly and positively and to allow each student the opportunities to make the most of his or her learning potential.

Addressing the diverse needs of our students increases the challenges that we face in higher education. This is especially true when we consider the unique qualities and needs of postsecondary learners (Rainey and Kolb 1995). Their diversity is increasingly greater because throughout our lives we develop our specific individual learning characteristics and traits. Our students are adults: they have developed and adapted in unique ways throughout their years in the educational system.

Yet, allowing for the differences among our students produces some valuable benefits. Not only do we help more of our students succeed, we improve our courses because our classes benefit from the diversity of our students, the variety of our approaches, and the dynamics promoted through a more positive environment.

As Schroeder (1993) states, it is important to understand that the population is not consistent. Fifty percent of the population needs to experience new information in a concrete, real way. This is contrary to how society generally gives/teaches new information. Society generally disseminates new information through the auditory mode. This is in stark contrast to the majority of the population. Therefore, it is important to look at the variety of approaches to the teaching and learning processes in order to assure that all aspects of the population are able to take in the information/data in a way that is preferable to them.

Learning Styles: A Brief Overview

A learning style is basically the preference or predisposition of an individual to perceive and process information in a particular way or combination of ways.

Learning styles can be analyzed and understood in various ways. Learning may be analyzed and understood according to the primary sense involved (visual, auditory, and tactile or kinesthetic), or according to psychological aspects of perception, or according to the method of processing information. Chapter 2 will present the basics of several of these approaches.

Learning can also be understood in terms of intelligences. Gardner (1983) has advanced the theory of multiple intelligences as areas of strength. He defines eight intelligences, as summarized in the following list (Campbell, Campbell, and Dickinson 1996):

- *Logical/mathematical:* ability to calculate, quantify, consider propositions and hypotheses, and do complex mathematical operations;

- *Linguistic:* ability to think in words and to use language to express and appreciate complex meanings;

- *Musical:* sensitivity to pitch, rhythm, and tone;

- *Spatial:* capacity to think in three-dimensional ways, to perceive imagery, to modify images, to move oneself or objects through space, and to understand how objects are related and how they fit together in an ordered manner;

- *Bodily/kinesthetic:* ability to manipulate objects and fine-tune physical skills;

- *Interpersonal:* capacity to understand and interact effectively with other people;

- *Intrapersonal:* ability to construct an accurate perception of oneself and to use such knowledge in planning and directing one's life.

- *Naturalist:* capacity to be sensitive to one's natural surroundings and perceive the world based upon these natural surroundings.

Every person has strengths in one or more of these areas. Although intelligence is not to be equated with learning style, there are some relationships and similarities.

Whether we consider learning in terms of perception, process or intelligences, one fact is indisputable: people learn in different ways. And within the perspective we may take to better understand the ways in which people learn there are many commonalities, which we will address throughout this book.

Four Steps to Teaching More Effectively

The first step for instructors is to understand how they themselves learn. The next step is to consider how they teach, in terms of how they learn. Then they can assess how each of their students learn and help them better understand themselves. As an instructor, it is critical to note at the outset that environmental factors substantially influence an individual student's learning style (Martin and Potter 1998). If the environmental factors do not match the individual learning style, then the student will not be successful. Finally they can teach more effectively by finding ways to accommodate their students' learning styles and help each of their students learn better.

Know Yourself: How Do You Learn?

Before instructors try to understand and accommodate their students' learning styles, they need to understand their own learning style. Like any other person, each instructor learns in specific ways, using specific techniques to perceive and process information.

Why is it important for instructors to know how they learn? Because we naturally tend to teach in ways that are consistent with how we learn. Even when an instructor seeks to emulate a favorite teacher from his or her years as a student, it's very likely that this favorite was somebody whose teaching style worked well with the learning style of the future instructor.

We all organize our thoughts, our responsibilities, and our lives in general according to the methods and processes with which we are comfortable. Two simple ways for instructors to understand their own unique learning style, which will then help them understand their students' learning styles, would be to perform these brief exercises.

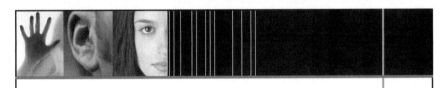

Tools for Identifying Learning Style

TASK #1

1. Think about one typical day in your life. What does it involve, both personally and professionally? Think of six typical tasks that you might have to remember to do in your personal life and/or your professional life.

2. Think about the process that you might use to remember to do these important tasks. Would you make a list? Would you memorize exactly what needs to be accomplished? Would you repeat the tasks over and over to yourself? Would you assign a number to each task in order to remember the total number of tasks as well as the tasks themselves?

3. Once you have considered the process that you typically use to accomplish tasks, share your process with a colleague who has also done steps 1 and 2 of this exercise.

4. Compare the processes you chose to accomplish your tasks. How are they similar? How are they different?

TASK #2

1. Think about a time when you are sitting in a meeting or a gathering with colleagues or friends. What is your stature? What do you find yourself doing during this meeting? Do you pay full attention or does your mind tend to wander?

2. Specific information is being disseminated in this meeting or gathering. How do you respond? Are you writing furiously? Are you doodling? Are you constantly asking questions? If you are finding yourself constantly asking questions, are these questions for additional facts or for clarification of information already given? Or do you just sit and listen?

3. Reflect on your behavior once the meeting or gathering is finished. Do you have the need to revisit or debrief the specifics of the meeting or gathering with another person? Do you merely go about your business and file the information from the meeting or gathering in your mind's Rolodex?

After completing this reflection task, discuss the information you have documented with a partner. Pay careful attention to conscious and unconscious choices of behaviors.

These exercises serve as a preliminary diagnostic tools to help instructors and students become more aware of differences in the ways in which they process information. For example, a person who makes a list of the tasks shows visual tendencies, while a person who repeats the tasks aloud is taking an auditory approach.

Something interesting to note here is that if people who are doing these simple exercises are encouraged to be precise about the processes that they use to remember tasks and the behaviors they implement as they participate in important gatherings, nuances emerge among their approaches. For example, one person may combine processes, perhaps making a list and also memorizing the tasks listed, while another person may think about the number of tasks and assign a number to each, in order to have a point of reference. Further, one person may choose to make a specific list of facts from a meeting, and another person may choose to doodle because they only choose to remember auditorily the key points of the gathering. When instructors understand their own learning styles, they are taking the first step toward beginning to understand how their students learn.

How Do You Teach?

The strategies that an instructor most commonly uses to teach are the strategies that he or she finds most comfortable in a learning situation.

If you tend to perceive things through an auditory mode, your teaching strategies are likely to emphasize hearing, the oral mode. If you tend to perceive things visually, your teaching strategies probably rely on what students can see, giving them a visual picture. If you tend to perceive things in tactile ways, your teaching strategies naturally would appeal to the touch, to movement.

Think back to some recent classes. How did you present new material to your students? What activities did you use to help them learn? By what methods did you determine how well they understood the material? Imagine those classes from the perspective of your students. What did they hear? What did they see? What did they touch? How did they move, if at all? What might their notes reveal about how you teach?

Remember that the primary purpose in understanding our own learning style and our students' learning styles, is to understand how we best take in information, how we best process information, and how we best use information and apply it. According to the auditory, visual, and tactile approach to learning styles, perception and the processing of information are indicators of what a student's preferred learning style may be.

When we reflect on how we teach, we usually realize that our teaching style is a combination of our learning style and the ways in which we were taught most successfully. But what works for us may not work for all of our students.

How Do Your Students Learn?

After we consider how we perceive and process information ourselves and how we teach, we can then focus on how our students learn best. We should know this in order to teach more effectively, and our students should know this in order to learn more effectively.

The benefits for our students extend beyond the classroom: they can apply what they know about how they learn not only to succeed in their courses, but also to the rest of their lives. This self-discovery is especially important for students who have been less successful in the educational system. This knowledge can produce positive psychological benefits. Many students gain self-esteem and feel more confident about themselves and their abilities when they understand how they learn and how they differ from their peers.

To help students learn about how they learn, Hand (1990) advocates debriefing during classroom or group sessions. Debriefing is a process in which the instructor provides feedback to a student and/or students provide feedback to each other. This allows the opportunity for all participants in the learning experience to discuss different approaches to solving problems, different solutions to tasks, and different strategies for learning. Thus, debriefing may give the instructor and the students insights into how they learn and may also expose the students to more effective strategies for learning, as each shares what might work for each individual.

How Can You Accommodate Learning Styles?

If we believe it is important that instructors prepare the learning environment so students can interact with it positively and have academic learning success, then we need to seek a good base of understanding when it comes to the teaching/learning process (Wolfe 2001).

In fact, it could be argued that teaching cannot be successful without knowledge of learning styles and a commitment to matching them with teaching styles and strategies.

This does not mean that an instructor needs to prepare 20 ways to teach the same thing. That would be completely unreasonable.

But it is important to make accommodations within individual lessons for the differences among the students in the group to allow every student the opportunity to learn as he or she learns best.

A common reaction to this multifaceted or holistic approach to teaching has been that it is impossible to vary strategies and activities regularly. Teaching in a holistic way requires that instructors vary teaching strategies on a consistent basis in order to touch the various learning styles regularly. An example of this is lecturing some of the time, organizing cooperative groups to discuss information, outlining course information/data, creating flow charts for course information and data, and having resources and materials for students to interact with. These examples of various teaching strategies should be part of the instructor's repertoire on a regular basis, thus assuring that different learning styles are addressed consistently. Sometimes it is a question of the content and goals of a particular course; sometimes it is a concern about the preparation that greater variety might require.

It should be noted, however, that the results are often worth the extra effort. Research supports the conclusion that students who have learned about their individual learning preferences, who have been taught to use a variety of strategies consistent with this learning preference, and who have had teachers who accommodated the preferences by adapting teaching strategies have made statistically significant increases in academic achievement (Dunn 1990).

Instructors are often concerned about motivation. It is a crucial factor in the learning process, yet most instructors acknowledge that it is simply not enough to expect their students to be internally motivated or motivated by the subject matter itself. We should organize lessons and activities with motivation in mind. It is easier to spark and maintain student interest when we appreciate their learning styles and try to reach every student. The results should be well worth the extra effort.

Finally, it is important for instructors to recognize and remember that there is no simple recipe for matching teaching strategies with learning styles. As we have noted, each person may have a unique combination of learning styles. Consequently, we should use a repertoire of strategies that span various learning styles.

Focus: Auditory, Visual, and Tactile/Kinesthetic

As we have stressed, there are many ways to understand how people learn: theories and approaches abound in educational psychology. The area of learning styles and intelligences can be confusing, as much by the similarities among the terms as by the differences in the theories.

The purpose of this book is to provide instructors with a simple, practical way to conceptualize how their students perceive and process information. Our approach is based on the primary sense involved in learning: visual, auditory, or tactile/kinesthetic.

This approach is based on behaviors, actions that instructors can readily perceive. The terms refer to the senses, which makes this approach easier to apply.

Although our focus in Chapters 4, 5, and 6 is on the auditory learner, the visual learner, and the tactile learner, respectively, these chapters make connections to other approaches, which are outlined in Chapter 2.

Adult Students: Nature and Experience

Teachers at all levels should understand at least the basics of learning styles. But those who work with postsecondary students must be especially aware of the differences among these styles and combinations. This is because of the ways in which learning styles develop.

Dunn (1990) explains that research shows that three-fifths of an individual's learning style is biological or genetic. Learning styles are influenced dramatically by personality. Personality traits and characteristics influence the ways in which we interact with our world, throughout our lives. Our experiences and society exert their influence: we adapt our learning processes and adopt strategies to succeed. Dewar (1996) and Hartman (1995) have found that students who become active participants in the learning process take ownership of their own personal achievement. These students become more self-motivated and become more conscious of their own learning success.

As the years pass, we establish a level of comfort and we learn how to cope or we have problems adapting to certain teaching strategies and we become frustrated, resigned to failure. By adulthood, we have fairly well developed our learning style. But we may not really understand how we learn or how we could learn better and more easily.

Hand (1990) states that if students can understand their individual learning styles, then they can begin to address different ways in which they can use various learning strategies for organizing material, doing assignments, studying, and taking tests.

Research into learning processes and learning styles as well as multiple intelligences raises important questions about strengths. It also raises even more important questions about weaknesses.

Just as every student of any age has a preferred learning style and can learn successfully when accommodated through appropriate teaching methods, there are learning styles with which each student is less comfortable. We have already considered the basic question about working with student learning strengths: if an instructor uses strategies compatible with the weaker learning styles, a student is less likely to learn as easily, and if an instructor uses strategies compatible with the strong learning style, a student is likely to learn more easily.

But there is a second question: whether instructors should also understand and acknowledge the weaker learning styles of their students and consciously implement strategies to strengthen those weaknesses.

Although it's more important, at least in the short term, to work with the strengths, it's also important, especially for long-term benefits, to strengthen the weaknesses. When students better learn how to develop their less-preferred learning styles, they can learn in a more holistic way. This may help them overcome the limitations of the specific learning styles.

If we use strategies that cross the various learning styles, we provide students with opportunities to become more adept at learning and help them develop their potential as more independent learners and more independent thinkers. Harb, Durrant, and Terry (1993) emphasize strategies that provide students with the whole picture. Providing a complete and conceptual view allows students to make connections to previous learning experiences and connect new information with information learned previously. Such connections will help students better understand the importance of the new information. Also, students learn how to make connections and to apply what they learn to the real world.

A natural way to expose students to ways of learning that may be less natural or comfortable for them is through group activities. Participation in diverse classroom groupings enables students to interact with students who use other learning styles and to learn from them.

Confusion, Misunderstandings, and Assumptions

There are many perspectives for understanding learning styles. The main focus of this book is to stress the necessity of applying what we know about them to postsecondary learning environments.

Research has established that learning styles are important. But research has also resulted in a multiplicity of perspectives and labels. This multiplicity makes this important area of research and application confusing.

Instructors may expect researchers to agree on one single approach to the learning process and to provide simple recipes for applying research findings in class. When they find a multitude of theories and perspectives and labels, they may be unable or unwilling to recognize the similarities and areas of consensus among the approaches, and they may miss the practical suggestions for accommodating learning styles. Consequently, they may not take advantage of the benefits of using what we know about learning styles to help their students succeed.

In this book, we attempt to give an overview of learning styles and to propose a particular approach to characterize learning styles as auditory, visual, and tactile/kinesthetic. This approach supports a holistic perspective of learning. This book offers practical ways for instructors to incorporate into their strategies what is known about learning differences, and it provides examples of typical student reactions. The intent of this guide is to help students experience greater success, both in school and beyond.

Conclusion

If we want to help our students succeed, we must understand how they learn and accommodate their individual differences. We cannot emphasize this enough. A major part of helping every student succeed is planning and implementing teaching strategies that span the variety of learning styles. Research shows the importance of understanding learning styles and of applying research findings to teaching in order to help all students succeed. As teachers embrace the learning styles approach to teaching, they should begin to see themselves as facilitators of learning, rather than merely disseminators of facts and data (Ojure and Sherman 2001). After teachers have the opportunity to read about and internalize information about the various learning styles, they begin to think about how to vary planning to accommodate these various learning styles. As they begin to experiment with multifaceted planning, they become more aware that the same concept can be presented in many different ways.

We need to be aware of the different approaches to learning styles and intelligences to better understand the differences in the ways in which individuals learn and how they perceive and process information. This is the purpose of Chapter 2, which provides a brief survey of the several theories to which the auditory, visual, and tactile styles are related in later chapters.

Chapter 3 discusses specific characteristics of the postsecondary learner, how these characteristics relate to learning styles, and how instructors can use these characteristics to teach more effectively and help all their students learn better.

Chapters 4, 5, and 6 discusses specific teaching strategies that address the individual learning needs of students according to visual, auditory, and tactile/kinesthetic learning style preferences, respectively. These chapters provide concrete examples for addressing the basic, individual learning needs of postsecondary learners and preparing the learning environment for all students to succeed.

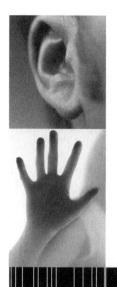

Tour of
Learning
Styles

CHAPTER TWO

This chapter provides a brief survey of the learning style theories that have influenced the perspective used in this book. This tour of learning styles summarizes the five theories proposed by Anthony F. Gregorc and Kathleen A. Butler; Ronald R. Sims and Serbrenia J. Sims; Bernice McCarthy; John N. Harb, S. Olani Durrant, and Ronald E. Terry; and Spence Rogers. It then shows how these theories have been synthesized into the approach used in this guide.

Anthony F. Gregorc
and Kathleen A. Butler

Gregorc (1985) and Butler (1988) use a theory that identifies style in terms of the labels Concrete, Abstract, Sequential, and Random. Gregorc and Butler believe that everyone can be classified into one or a combination of these styles. Gregorc further believes that it is the mission of every teacher to help students with the task of increasing self-knowledge. Gregorc also believes that in this quest for self-knowledge, it is a teacher's responsibility to assist students to heighten their depth of awareness of others. In understanding oneself, we as learners can verbalize what learning and teaching situation we may need. In understanding others, as teachers we can consciously arrange the learning environment to address individual learning needs.

Concrete learners need to be involved in learning a concept in a very real way. As much as possible, concrete learners need situations in which they can have concrete objects, manipulatives, and the like that will make learning real for them. It is critical for these learners to be physically involved with a new concept or new information.

Abstract learners tend to be precise and attentive to specific details. These learners can take pieces of data and synthesize them together to understand concepts as wholes. Abstract learners are cognitive by nature.

Sequential learners are structured and ordered. The learning process for these learners needs to be clear and precise. Specific details need to be clearly delineated, and concrete steps have to be specifically outlined.

Random learners are holistic by nature. They are not ordered or structured, and they cannot operate in a structured way in learning situations or life's situations. They prefer to be diffused in their attempt to understand something new. They learn in a holistic and global manner.

Gregorc and Butler believe that people approach learning and life in general in these four ways. They also believe that people could have tendencies in a combination of areas, but with definite preferences. For this reason, it is important for instructors to understand which style is a student's preference. Once an instructor has determined the learning preference, it is then easier to plan appropriate lessons with learning success in mind.

Ronald R. Sims and Serbrenia J. Sims

Sims and Sims (1995c) propose a learning styles theory that addresses the individual's processing perspective. They attempt to understand how someone might process new information in order to best understand it, using the classifications Cognitive, Affective, Perceptual, and Behavioral.

A person with a *Cognitive* learning preference will process information in pieces or parts, in a way similar to Gregorc and Butler's Abstract or Sequential learner. The person with the Cognitive preference needs to understand specific parts of a new concept before comprehending the whole concept. It is also important for people with a Cognitive preference to have adequate thinking time and an ordered pattern for this thinking. This ordered pattern of thinking involves understanding a concept in a sequential way.

The *Perceptual* learner will tend to process information from the point of view of what a concept seems to be. The Perceptual person will attempt to understand a new concept by looking at the concept holistically and analyzing the pieces of the concept from a holistic viewpoint going from the whole to its parts. The Perceptual learner needs a visual aid as a learning tool in order to get the whole picture. The Perceptual learner attempts to understand a new concept by using the senses in a holistic way. This type of learner is similar to Gregorc and Butler's Random/Concrete learner. The concrete aspect of the learning style requires a visual to make a concept real; the random aspect is in the Perceptual learner's attempt to look at all aspects of a concept holistically.

The *Behavioral* learner needs to be doing, to be physically involved in interacting with a new concept in order to comprehend it. This approach is similar to the Concrete style in Gregorc and Butler's theory.

The *Affective* learner brings feelings and emotions to the learning situation. This approach could be compared to the holistic learner, the Random learner, and the Perceptual learner, who make sense or comprehend something new by understanding all aspects of it.

Bernice McCarthy

McCarthy (1990) places people in quadrants based upon different characteristics. It can be inferred that these characteristics are related to the way people might process information and learn as they progress through life. In her 4MAT Learning Styles Wheel, she uses adjectives such as Analytic and Imaginative and Dynamic/Common Sensible as descriptors for different learning styles.

The *Analytic* learner processes information in pieces. This can be related to Gregorc and Butler's Abstract and Sequential learner. Analytic learners understand new concepts and information best in an empirical way, in which respect they are similar to Sims and Sims's Cognitive learner. They are best with facts and individual pieces of data, which they eventually put together to understand holistic concepts.

The *Imaginative* learner relies on the creative visions he or she can invent in the process of pictorial imaging in the mind's eye. This type of learner imagines a new concept in a holistic way and imagines this new concept with every aspect represented. In this way, imaginative learners create a visual image, either in their minds or in a format such as a chart, graph, or diagram. This Imaginative learner is similar to Gregorc and Butler's Random/Concrete learner in that he or she creates holistic concepts and requires something concrete, such as a mental image or a graphic format. This type of learner is also similar to Sims and Sims's perceptual learner in that he or she uses the senses or sensory experiences to make sense of a new concept.

Chart One: 4MAT Learning Styles Wheel

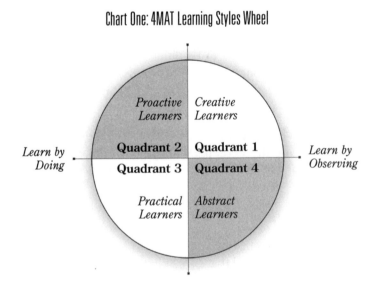

The *Dynamic/Common Sensible* learner has to learn in a very active way. To make sense of new information, this type of learner needs to be actively involved in seeking it out and manipulating it. These learners are practical by nature and interact with the practical aspects of information that they are attempting to understand. These Dynamic/Common Sensible learners are similar to Gregorc and Butler's Concrete learners and to Sims and Sims's Behavioral/Affective learners. These learners need to more "physically" interact with new information in order to understand and master it fully. Also, they bring their feelings to the learning process.

John N. Harb, S. Olani Durrant, and Ronald E. Terry

Harb, Durrant, and Terry (1993) classify learners according to three categories: Reflective/Abstract, Concrete, and Active.

The *Reflective/Abstract* learner needs time to ponder information. This type of learner takes in pieces of information and considers such aspects as relationships, connections, and possible influences of the different pieces on each other. He or she then puts all the pieces together in order to understand a concept. The reflection time allows the opportunity for adequate processing. It is through this reflective processing that this type of learner is able to master concepts. This Reflective/Abstract learner is similar to Gregorc and Butler's Abstract/Sequential learner, Sims and Sims's Cognitive learner, and McCarthy's Analytic learner.

The *Concrete* learner needs to see things in order to understand them. To grasp a new concept or learn new information, these learners need a concrete visual so they can see things in a global way to understand all the parts of the concept or information. This Concrete learner is similar to Gregorc and Butler's Concrete/Random learner in his or her need to see things and to do so holistically. These learners are also similar to Sims and Sims's Perceptual learner in that they use their senses to understand a concept, to make sense of something new, which they do in a holistic, global way. The Concrete learner is similar to McCarthy's Imaginative learner in that he or she creates images to make sense of an experience, images that serve as learning tools.

The *Active* learner needs to control the learning. He or she needs to make sense of the information for himself or herself. This type of learner is similar to Gregorc and Butler's Concrete learner and to Sims and Sims's Behavioral learner.

Spence Rogers

Rogers (1999) looks at learners in terms of how they attempt to control learning for their own life processes. Everything learners do has a goal of making sense of information and understanding it so they can use it in their own lives. Rogers believes that learning is a cycle. This cycle should always begin with experience, lead to some type of thinking about or reflecting on the information and/or data from this experience, and later having an application phase of this information and/or data. This application phase is critical in that only at this point has a learner mastered the information/data well enough to use it in another situation or learning experience. Rogers takes Kolb's theory and applies the different learning styles to include the reflection piece.

Additionally, Rogers feels that students should have information chunked together and never have more than seven ideas/pieces of information presented at once. Monitoring the amount of information presented allows for the reflection time that Rogers believes assists with the learning process.

Last, Spence Rogers believes in the physical aspect of learning. Movement is critical, according to Rogers. He presents his learning theory from the perspective that students should be allowed to move consistently during the presentation of concepts, and that a way for students to really learn and understand these concepts is for them to associate where they were located physically when they learned the concept to the concept itself.

The Synthesis: Lynne M. Celli Sarasin

The focus of this book is to address the learning needs of students from a perspective that considers their preferences in terms of Auditory, Visual, and Tactile/Kinesthetic. This perspective takes into account the theories presented previously and attempts to synthesize the characteristics defined in those theories into an approach that can be easily translated into strategies in a college or university classroom setting.

Auditory learners need information to be presented orally. They also prefer information to be presented as individual facts in order to first understand those facts thoroughly and then eventually understand the whole concept.

Auditory learners can think abstractly. They tend to be reflective, sequential, and analytic, and they are cognitive by nature.

Visual learners require visual aids in order to make sense of something new. These visuals can be drawings, charts, diagrams, or outlines. They can also be mental images. In fact, visual learners often form mental images as a strategy to cope with learning situations that do not meet their learning style needs.

Visual learners have characteristics that are random, holistic, global, perceptual, concrete, and imaginative. They prefer to learn about a concept completely before trying to understand its parts, and they use their senses throughout the learning process.

Tactile/Kinesthetic learners learn by doing. They rely on physical interaction during the learning process. They need to be active and dynamic participants in order to fully understand something new. They are behavioral by nature and need to do something in order to understand the nuances or truly master a concept. They are concrete by nature and prefer manipulatives. If Tactile/Kinesthetic learners are engaged in active learning, they will master the concept and be able to apply the concept to other situations.

Chart Two: Characteristics of Learners				
Celli Sarasin	Gregorc/Butler	Sims & Sims	McCarthy	Harb, Durrant & Terry
Auditory	Abstract/ Sequential	Cognitive	Analytic	Abstract/ Reflective
Visual	Random/ Concrete	Perceptual	Imaginative	Concrete
Tactile	Concrete	Behavioral/ Affective	Dynamic	Active/ Concrete

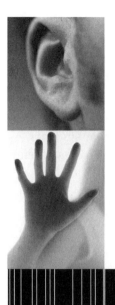

Postsecondary Students and Learning Styles

CHAPTER THREE

Expertise in a discipline does not necessarily give a person the skills necessary to teach well. Postsecondary instructors need to know about strategies, methods, and assessment, both of learning and of teaching. They also need, as we have stressed, to understand about learning styles and about postsecondary students in particular. According to Martin and Potter (1998), learning styles might have several different aspects. They too agree that learning styles look carefully at how a person takes in information, processes through that information, and later is able to apply that information and use it in future situations.

Assumptions About Postsecondary Learners

Knowles and colleagues (1984) have underscored the importance of understanding certain assumptions that educators have made about postsecondary learners, both in teaching and in research involving these students. More than ever postsecondary students are enthusiastic to fulfill obligations of high education and need to be armed with strategies that will assure their success in real world situations.

- Postsecondary students are highly motivated to learn because they have an orientation to life different from that of younger students. As adults, they have had experiences that they can use as points of reference for new information to which they are exposed.

- Many postsecondary learners have a work-centered attitude. They want information that they can apply to real life. The academic disciplines that are the most relevant are the disciplines in which postsecondary learners will most likely excel.

- Experience is the richest source for postsecondary learning. Experiential learning is extremely successful for postsecondary learners. Some academic disciplines are less easily learned experientially. But, whenever possible, information should be presented using examples of how that information can be translated into the real world.

- Postsecondary students are goal oriented. They are practical and tend to be problem solvers. Therefore, lessons and activities should be designed with problem solving in mind.

- Lessons and presentations should be self-directed, if possible. Because the postsecondary learner is generally motivated and industrious, lessons that encourage students to take ownership of learning and decision making about how to learn are the most successful. Also, postsecondary learners tend to be competency oriented. They need to be taught skills that have a meaning in their circumstances and information that can be applied in practical ways.

- It is critical to acknowledge that individual differences increase with age, including differences in learning styles. Adult learners have developed strategies to learn better, sometimes to adapt to a variety of teaching styles through their years in the educational system.

Awareness of these assumptions about postsecondary learners will help instructors plan, use, and assess teaching methods that effectively accommodate a variety of learning styles.

Helping Postsecondary Students Learn

When interpreting research about postsecondary learners, it is important to understand the data in terms of the learning process and in terms of the goals.

Learning should provide long-term benefits. Real learning means that information and skills will be used throughout life. Therefore, when planning learning activities, instructors should keep in mind long-term benefits rather than immediate results. Students should be learning for life, not just for an exam and a grade. Learning for life is when a student can make the learning bridge and apply his or her knowledge to situations in life and make these situations meaningful. A teaching strategy that helps make information meaningful within a learning situation naturally helps with the learning bridge and the practical application of whatever has been learned in the classroom (Hickcox 1995).

It is important to provide postsecondary students with information or skills that are easily applied to the real world so they will understand the importance of the learning experience. Instructors need to reinforce this learning bridge to help their students realize the relevance of what they are learning. For some students, the reason for learning something may not be as evident as it is for others. Instructors need to emphasize the reasons for all learning activities and tie them to the practical side of the real world. This is especially true for postsecondary learners.

Students Who Learn Actively, Instructors Who Facilitate

Postsecondary learners should be active participants whenever possible, rather than passive recipients (Sheal 1989). It's important for instructors to think of themselves as facilitators. This approach encourages identifying with students experiences and opinions in setting learning goals and objectives and in planning activities.

Facilitation has proven to be more effective than lecturing (Zemke and Zemke 1995). Beyond the lecture, the possibilities are overwhelming (Sims 1995c) discussions, laboratory experiences, workshops, experiential learning situations, problem-centered seminars, programmed instruction, mastery learning.

Our first step is to consider some points about postsecondary learning and teaching in general. Then we will focus on the significance of learning styles.

Learning Environment

Knowles and colleagues (1984) summarize the important points to remember when planning for successful learning experiences for post-secondary students.

The first step is to set the environment to make it conducive for learning, both physically and psychologically.

The physical aspects of the learning environment send specific messages to the students about what learning means and how they are expected to act. The organization is especially important. Postsecondary learners will be less motivated in a structured environment, with the desks in rows, for example, than in a configuration that arranges the desks into smaller clusters, a configuration more suitable for cooperative learning and group problem solving.

The environment should be flexible. It should also promote trust. This is important for any learning but especially for learning how to learn. Instructors should encourage respect, trust, openness, support, and collaboration. When this is the case, students will be positively motivated to participate in new learning situations.

Instructors should always plan activities with specific intentions in mind. The students can understand these activities better and participate in them more actively if their instructor explains the purposes and procedures. It is especially important in new situations to explain the objectives and to provide instructions and guidelines that are specific and clear. Students are more likely to participate with enthusiasm and confidence if they understand why they are doing an activity and what is expected of them. This understanding plants seeds of motivation and sometimes even sparks the self-motivation levels in students (Zemke and Zemke 1995).

Some postsecondary students are also motivated by an atmosphere of competition, but this sort of motivation is not necessarily healthy or effective in terms of real learning and long-term benefits. More important, competition generally hurts most students, especially those who have not succeeded in competitive classrooms throughout their years in elementary and secondary education.

Postsecondary learners are generally better motivated when they feel that the information they are acquiring and the skills they are developing will be useful and relevant, when what they are learning fits their needs (Knowles 1988). They will also be motivated by success, which will boost their self-esteem. This is particularly true for students who have had trouble in earlier learning environments.

Lessons or activities must be designed to maximize success and build self-esteem, a vital component of the learning process and a positive force that translates into every other aspect of the student's life. Instructors should understand the value of motivating through success and plan opportunities for each student to succeed and to be an active participant in the learning process. This active participation allows students to take control of their own learning and be at the center of the learning process (Hunter and McCants 1977).

Instructors can also help motivate their students by showing them that the information or skills will be useful to them right away, an important incentive, as we have previously suggested.

Instructors can also increase motivation by arousing curiosity. One important way to do this is through questions that challenge the students to wonder, to think, to investigate, and to discuss. Questions that stimulate critical thinking, challenge assumptions or beliefs, or encourage students to develop hypotheses or draw conclusions are the types of questions that excite curiosity and support more active participation in the learning process.

To expand their repertoire of learning strategies, students need opportunities and time to try new strategies and to gain experience with other ways of learning. This necessarily involves taking risks. Students who feel comfortable in their learning environment and motivated by positive factors such as we have discussed will be more likely to learn how to learn and to enjoy the experiences.

Strategies for Active Learning

Because postsecondary students will learn better if they are involved actively in the learning process, it is important for instructors to plan activities such as the following:

- Role-playing
- Case studies

- Debates, discussion, and civil disagreements that represent diverse perspectives

- Problem-solving in situations where there might be several solutions

Such activities help keep the learning environment varied and exciting, motivate and involve the students, and focus on higher-order cognitive skills.

Instructors can plan situations with goals or objectives that encourage debate and diverse perspectives. In planning, however, they should anticipate how they might monitor such situations, perhaps by questioning the students, so that they clarify the students' ideas or develop their perspectives.

It is also important to be prepared to take a learning situation in different directions. If the students discuss certain perspectives, instructors should be ready with appropriate information and resources to support and promote that discussion as it develops.

Any real learning requires reflection, the opportunity for the students to process what they are learning. Reflection is especially important for more active learning activities. To ensure that students have this opportunity and that they understand the importance of reflection, instructors should build reflection time into the classroom or group time.

Often instructors may view this as taking time away from "real learning," leaving less time to cover new material. However, merely covering material provides no guarantee that the students are really learning that material or that they can use it. Postsecondary students need ample opportunity to practice and use new skills and new information or they are less likely to retain those skills and that information.

During the reflection time incorporated into these types of activities, students must also have time for interactive feedback, whether between student and instructor or among students. This allows the students an opportunity for questions and clarifications and gives them additional time to practice. This feedback, or what Hand (1990) terms debriefing, is critical: it allows the students to experience the learning process with someone guiding them. The guidance, feedback, or debriefing process gives each student a regular confirmation of how he or she is understanding the material or developing the skills.

This sort of interaction allows students who need to talk about new material in order to completely process it the opportunity to do so. Adding this component to the learning process gives students an additional mode of processing information, which may better accommodate their individual learning styles and needs. This interaction also gives the instructor a sense of how students are learning and which areas need special attention.

As they plan their activities, instructors need to try to incorporate time for students to engage in these interactive learning experiences.

Rainey and Kolb (1995) recommend personal reaction assignments as a regular part of the classroom learning situation. In these assignments, both instructor and students should react to the classroom structure, teaching assignments, and teaching strategies. Students should react to the correspondence between teaching strategies and assignments and their learning style preferences, as well as reacting generally to course content and its applicability for use outside the class or group setting. This sharing of reactions will help both instructor and students arrange situations that better meet individual learning and help maintain open communication between instructor and students. This then becomes a natural part of the ongoing process by which the instructor and the students better understand how the students learn most effectively.

Abstract versus Conceptual

Many postsecondary instructors seem to assume that their students are fully capable of abstract learning. Certainly, the course content at that level often tends to be abstract by nature. Some instructors may teach in abstract terms, putting content first, above applicability to reality or even comprehension.

But postsecondary instructors need to include among their teaching strategies activities that allow students opportunities to enter into learning situations that are concrete and that students readily understand. Although sometimes characterized as adult learners, first-year college students, especially those recently in high school, prefer concrete experiences rather than abstract experiences (Purkiss 1994). They may not understand concepts that do not seem grounded in reality or seem to have no applicability for them.

Such students often experience difficulty adapting and succeeding. Teaching styles that are abstract and conceptual, rather than experiential, put these students at a disadvantage relative to their peers who have experience with abstract and conceptual teaching. Commonly, postsecondary instructors teach only to the few students who have had abstract and conceptual experiences, while the other students lag behind, confused and usually not motivated to learn.

Students at the postsecondary level need to participate in experiential learning experiences because most have had little exposure to abstract and conceptual content and teaching and often little success and because many naturally learn better and more easily through experiential activities.

Again, it should be emphasized that students need to understand the relevance of the information and skills they are learning because they are primarily preparing for the real world. Their educational experiences must include practical applications of information and skills in order for the students to be motivated in the formal learning situation.

The natural extension of this experiential approach is the internship. This real world experience allows students the opportunity to use their new information and skills and better understand their relevance.

Learning ... and Learning How to Learn

As we emphasize throughout this book, an integral part of the learning process for postsecondary students should be learning how to learn, developing strategies that will help them acquire information and skills in college and beyond.

In most new situations in life, we tend to use what has worked for us in the past. Our students behave similarly in learning situations.

We should remember that, just as with information and skills, students will master new learning strategies only if they have enough time to use them in a variety of situations and become comfortable with them. We should specifically plan opportunities for students to use new learning strategies so that our students work with them enough to eventually use them on their own.

Postsecondary students generally prefer learning information one chunk at a time so they can really understand each chunk and relate it to what they already know. Instructors should summarize often to help their students understand how to synthesize what they have learned. Synthesizing promotes memory recall and long-term retention of information by encouraging students to process and assimilate what they learn within the context of what they know. In this process, it's essential for instructors to help their students work with the material in whatever ways best suit their ways of learning.

Students should have adequate time both to process and apply new information and to develop and use new skills. Once students have been exposed to information, experientially if possible, and have had time to reflect on the new material, they need to see how it connects and applies with what they already know. It is important for instructors to provide students with a chance to create concepts and connections and to integrate their reflections, observations, concepts, and information.

Allowing students time to create concepts and connections is an important component of the application process. Students need to take what they know and understand and use this information in other ways and in other situations. This is one of the most critical parts of the learning process for postsecondary learners. They need to feel that what they are learning will be useful to them in the real world, and they need to be able to use the new knowledge and skills in different ways.

Instructors need to build this application process into their plans to ensure that students are understanding not only the course content but also the learning process (Kolb 1984).

Kolb states that students need to engage in a wide variety of new experiences, which should include opportunities to reflect upon new information, use that information, and consider how the information affects how they understand a new concept. Once students have participated in such experiences involving reflection and application in the classroom or group setting, they should then also have extensive opportunities to create new concepts from the new information. This phase provides them with opportunities to synthesize, evaluate, and apply information that they have learned, which makes learning real for them and extends the process. An example of this process might be the opportunity for students to take information learned about theories of educational instruction and create a unit of study to be implemented in practicum setting. Use of the theories of education in planning should be highlighted and easily identifiable so the instructor can document the transfer of information. In a similar way, marketing students could also take information learned surrounding sound business practices and create their own small business. As in the education example, the theories of sound business practices should be easily identifiable by the instructor.

Application of the concepts—concepts with which they have worked and concepts that they have created—is a critical step in the learning process. In fact, it is the essence of that process: without application, students experiences in the classroom or group setting exist in a void, remaining in the learning situation. If not applied, this learning is without purpose.

Instructors must make sure that experiences with the application of new concepts and information are a part of the normal learning environment. They need to plan for these application experiences and provide them regularly. Merely knowing information is not enough: real learning means being able to use what is learned.

Beyond Content and Learning Strategies

We should also help our students in areas beyond course content and learning strategies. Specific skills to be emphasized with postsecondary learners are those that address individual learning styles and those that are needed to succeed in life: decision-making skills, leadership skills, and problem-solving skills (Sims 1995).

With proper planning, instructors in almost any academic discipline can help their students of all learning styles develop these skills and experience success using them. Activities that involve using specific skills in general ways help students learn to transfer those skills to the real world.

For example, the classroom or group environment must be organized to incorporate specific information with activities that encourage and help develop problem-solving and leadership skills. A classroom lesson may include learning specific concepts, but a cooperative learning activity may help develop leadership skills because it helps students master specific content. It is the instructor's responsibility to plan appropriately so students have experience with both specific discipline skills and general skills that can be used in real life.

We can also help our students learn how to learn by asking them more sophisticated questions, to encourage higher-order thinking and application of information and skills. A basic guide in this area is the taxonomy of cognitive objectives (Bloom 1956). (There are also taxonomies of objectives for the affective and psychomotor domains.) This taxonomy, which provides a general frame of reference for teaching strategies and learning activities, can help instructors ask questions appropriate to their objectives.

There are six levels of objectives:

1. Knowledge

2. Comprehension

3. Application

4. Analysis

5. Synthesis

6. Evaluation

At Level 1, you want your students to acquire new knowledge. Your questions would ask them to recall memorized information facts, terms, formulas, principles, and so forth.

At Level 2, you want your students to use the information to interpret or extrapolate from it. Your questions might ask them to rephrase what they have learned, to summarize, to make comparisons, to draw conclusions, or to otherwise show that they have understood.

At Level 3, you want your students to put to use what they know. If you want them to solve problems, for example, you might ask questions to lead them through the process to identify the known and unknown elements of the problem, to structure these elements according to a known model, to choose a method or principle that allows them to solve the problem, and then to solve the problem using that method or applying that principle.

At Level 4, you want your students to take apart a specific idea or body of knowledge. You would use questions that focus on breaking down the whole into parts, identifying the relationships that exist among these parts, and revealing the underlying principles of organization.

At Level 5, you want to help your students develop their abilities to express themselves and to think independently. You would ask questions to elicit personal reactions, opinions, and thoughts and to show a sense of creative activity using information that the students have learned.

At Level 6, you want your students to use their critical sense to evaluate ideas to which they have been exposed or work that they have done. You would ask questions that lead them to judge, to show expertise that involves skills developed at the lower levels (knowledge, comprehension, application, analysis, and synthesis).

We should help our students understand new ideas or new concepts through activities that are realistic, encourage the students to think critically, and challenge them to take risks in using information and skills in new learning situations. Each and every task should contain an element of challenge. However, this challenge should not be too great, or students will fear failure and not be as motivated to participate in the learning experience.

To help students learn about how they learn, instructors should encourage them to verbalize their learning process. This verbalization provides them with the opportunity to reflect upon a learning situation and think about what helped them learn and how it helped, as well as about what was not useful. This reflection may help them determine which strategies to use in other learning contexts (Stouch 1993). Some students may even need to go as far as to make visual pictures in their mind about the steps in their learning process. They may have to actually visualize themselves in each specific step of the learning process in order to better understand the steps they go through. As the instructor, you may need to ask focus questions to facilitate the students in this process. Questions that require the students to be reflective and articulate specific behaviors during a task will assist to this end.

Students need to know themselves and understand how they learn in order to honestly assess the effectiveness of learning situations and the effectiveness of teaching strategies. Throughout this process, student and instructor will bring into focus that student's individual learning style and the best learning situations that accommodate that style. Once they begin this process of referencing preferential learning situations, students will begin to readily take advantage of learning situations that they believe will allow them to succeed.

At this point in the process, students should be able to articulate their individual learning needs in terms of preferable teaching strategies. Their instructors should be open to those needs; if the students have been participating in this process thus far, ongoing analysis will be a natural component. Communication is critical throughout this process: students should communicate their learning needs and the instructor should communicate appropriate teaching strategies and learning activities.

Feedback between instructor and student, as well as student and student, guides the students in their journey of learning. The instructor articulates and reinforces basic expectations and learning goals, but the students are able to explore their own learning goals.

The students need to know what they are attempting to accomplish and to what extent they are meeting their goals on an ongoing basis. They should also analyze their own learning needs. This task involves compromising between their individual needs and the formal or prescribed learning. This task may be difficult, if the individual needs require that the teaching and learning situation deviate from the formal or prescribed learning situation, especially if that situation has been the status quo.

Part of encouraging students to analyze their learning needs is to have them develop their own learning objectives in conference with their instructor. Next, all students and their instructors should together be involved in planning so they share ownership of the decisions affecting the learning situation.

Knowles and colleagues (1984) articulate a four-step process to allow students to develop their own learning objectives:

- The learner puts the learning needs into a learning objective format.

- The learner points out resources that will help meet those learning objectives.

- The learner develops a formula that includes evidence that this learning has taken place—some sort of evaluation tool.

- The learner decides how the evidence of learning will be used for future evaluation and planning.

These four steps have traditionally been the responsibility of the instructor. However, it serves the postsecondary learner well to be equally involved in this process. It is critical that we enable our students to develop individual learning plans, carry these plans to fruition, and evaluate their own learning. Active involvement in the whole process is the key to success for postsecondary learners.

Each student will be most likely to learn best in situations that address his or her individual learning needs. During this process, students need to review and analyze their specific learning process with reference to different learning situations. In this review, they can benefit from feedback and other assistance from instructors and peers, which may help them better understand their approach to learning and thus help them learn more successfully. In this referencing process, students and instructors participate in the learning process and observe that process to better understand how each individual learns most effectively.

Learning-How-To-Learn

Stouch (1993) believes that there are three parts to what she terms the Learning-How-To-Learn concept. Both instructors and students need to understand the parts of this critical concept in order for the learning process, as a whole, to be successful.

The first part is knowing about the learning process itself. Self-awareness, understanding how the memory operates, and general knowledge about learning are important parts of this first step of understanding learning as a whole process. Once instructors and students understand the learning process itself, they can apply this knowledge in various learning situations, such as self-directed learning, collaborative learning, and group learning.

The second part of understanding the learning process is knowing about learning styles. Once students understand certain aspects of individual learning styles, they will be able to request the type of information or teaching strategy they need to succeed in a learning situation. Once learners understand their individual learning style, they will be able to try out different strategies that may not be as comfortable to them. This practice will expand their ability to learn.

The third part is for instructors to provide ways for students to improve their learning proficiency. They can do this by incorporating strategies that encourage their students to know about the learning process as well as by understanding and testing out their own learning styles and others and by providing opportunities for their students to practice their skills (Stouch 1993).

Because learning about learning involves changing and adapting, it is part of the instructor's responsibility to encourage and help students make the necessary changes and adaptations.

Psychological Contract

Rainey and Kolb (1995) state that the instructor and the student need to make a psychological contract. They should establish this psychological contract from the start. They should state and understand their expectations and articulate their learning and teaching preferences. Much if this contract is articulated in the course syllabus. For smaller classes, the discussion of the syllabus can involve students and instructors debating course requirements and strategies that will be used during the class. For larger classes, the syllabus becomes and even more important part of the contract. Postsecondary instructors need to acknowledge that much of the contract between themselves and their students lies within this document. Therefore, the syllabus must be clear and the teaching and learning strategies varied and communicated as such.

Even in larger institutions, instructors and students can arrive at an understanding of these expectations and preferences through in-depth interviews, ongoing dialogue, and verbal exchanges of what the instructor and the student have observed of the learning process. At larger institutions this can be a bit more difficult, but it still can be accomplished if students are serious about understanding their learning processes and expectations of their instructors.

The psychological contract, as defined within the syllabus, should set classroom behavior guidelines for both instructor and student. These guidelines should help the instructor and the student understand their goals and expectations and reinforce their mutual respect. To help maintain this psychological contract, there should be continued dialogue. If expectations and/or behavior guidelines need to be modified or changed, this should be discussed.

Understanding and Using Learning Styles

The first part of this chapter has been devoted to postsecondary students and their learning environment in general. We now move to a consideration of how to understand and use learning styles in four basic steps.

The first step is for the instructor to take definitive steps to identify how his or her students learn. The next step is to empower the students to understand their own learning styles. Then, the instructor should use this knowledge in planning and implementing learning experiences. Finally, the instructor must help his or her students expand their scope of learning. Although each student may learn best in a certain way, each student should also be exposed to a variety of learning experiences to become a more versatile learner and to better prepare for the real world. Further, Darling-Hammond (1997), states that all learning activities should be arranged with the students' needs in mind. If students need independence during the learning process this should be kept in mind when preparing lessons and activities.

What Are Learning Styles?

As we noted in Chapter 1, we use the term learning style to mean a certain pattern of behavior in approaching a learning experience, taking in new information, developing new skills, and retaining that new information and those new skills. Understanding learning styles includes understanding how students approach a learning experience, how they learn from that experience, how they evaluate the experience, and how they apply new information and skills to situations in life. Additionally, the definition of learning styles includes the way a person processes, internalizes, and concentrates on new information (Gremli 1996). Gremli further states that people find it easier when they receive information or data the same way they process it (i.e., receive information visually, process information visually). As Keefe and Jenkins (2002) state, learning styles are generally how a student prefers to learn. They speak of a student profile that encompasses three categories relative to learning: cognitive style, affective style, and physiological style.

Understanding Individual Cognitive Style

A natural next step in understanding this concept of learning styles is understanding individual cognitive style, because cognitive style plays an important role in the development of a student's learning style. Cognitive style simply is how a person processes information.

When instructors and students can identify and articulate the processes that the students use to represent information, solve problems, remember information, and carry out other operations, they can then understand what has worked and how they can build upon that success. This makes it easier for instructors to understand their students, their needs, and their individual learning styles.

Sims and Sims (1995a) state that the working definition of learning style should include the different ways in which people behave and should recognize that different people feel in different ways, process information differently, and behave differently in varied learning situations.

As we noted in Chapter 1, research shows that our learning styles are three-fifths biological or genetic, strongly influenced by personality characteristics inherited from our biological parents (Dunn 1990). Yet, as Kolb (1984) states learning styles are also developmental.

They develop as a result of learning experiences, and they continue to change throughout life. As people grow and mature and participate in learning experiences, their individual learning styles will grow and develop according to these experiences.

However, it is important to note that it does not matter how many learning experiences a student has that may not be compatible with his or her primary learning style. Those learning experiences will not change his or her preferred learning style.

Influences on Learning Style

It is important to acknowledge that there are environmental influences that play a part in learning preference. For example, some students can study and/or learn with music playing, while others need complete silence. The amount of stimuli that a person can accept and still learn successfully is a characteristic of that person's learning style. The amount of learning will increase if the amount of outside stimuli matches the amount that a certain learning style requires or can accept.

For example, an auditory learner may be able to tolerate outside stimuli, while a visual learner may be bothered by such stimuli.

Personality can also influence learning style. For example, a very outgoing and social student may need interaction with others to process information adequately enough to apply it, while a more reserved student may learn better away from other students.

As noted earlier, we should understand the learning styles of postsecondary students in terms of the effects of their earlier learning experiences. Whatever learning style(s) may be natural to a particular student, that student has learned in other ways, perhaps very successfully, perhaps less successfully, and developed strategies and attitudes that also affect how he or she learns at the postsecondary level.

Even though students can adapt, sometimes deceptively well, to educational systems and strategies that are at odds with their learning styles, we must not simply believe that they can ignore those learning styles that students will come to learn best in the manner to which they have had the most exposure. They may adapt, yes, but not learn best.

This is especially true for adult learners because of their many years of various learning situations. Therefore, we need to acknowledge that each of our students has a specific, preferred learning style that is well developed.

Other Tendencies

We also need to acknowledge and understand certain tendencies that affect how our students learn. Two important tendencies in the current research are the continua of dependent/independent and global/analytical.

Learners are sometimes labeled as independent or dependent. Both dependent and independent learners are found in any given classroom, and neither type is necessarily better or more successful than the other within a learning situation.

Independent learners have an analytical approach to learning: they are able to perceive the individual parts of a concept. They are achievement-oriented, competitive, self-motivated, active, autonomous, able to analyze information, and likely to have longer attention spans (Keefe and Thompson 1987). Independent learners prefer formal learning situations; they need specific learning objectives, lecture outlines, and planned activities. Inherent organization of tasks and materials is critical for independent learners.

Dependent learners have a more comprehensive approach to learning: they are able to perceive concepts as wholes. They tend to be global learners, attentive to social cues, easily distracted, and comfortable in informal learning situations (Keefe and Thompson 1987). Dependent learners rely heavily on their sensory modes to understand experiences. They tend to need to keep their hands or whole bodies busy, and they are interested in the outside stimuli.

More comparisons of these concepts and how they relate to learning styles will be discussed in the next three chapters as we consider the styles of auditory, visual, and tactile learners. However, this research about independent and dependent learners underscores the importance for instructors to organize the environment so that both types of learners have the opportunity to succeed.

Postsecondary learners can also be labeled as global or analytical. Although these labels have been used in research in conjunction with other approaches, some researchers use only the global-analytical continuum to attempt to understand learning styles and individual learning processes.

A global learner tends to approach a learning task from a holistic perspective. This learner looks at a concept as a whole concept from the beginning. As this learner progresses through the learning process, he or she becomes aware of the different parts of the concept.

The best strategies for helping global learners will include holistic presentation of new information. For them, learning experiences should introduce information conceptually, rather than as individual facts.

An analytical learner, on the other hand, prefers to approach a learning task by interacting with pieces of information, fact by fact. He or she needs to understand individual pieces of information in order to eventually understand the whole concept.

The best strategies for helping analytical learners will address the individual parts of a whole concept and will allow students time during presentations to understand and master those parts.

Confusion Over Learning Styles and Labels

Because researchers have defined the concept of learning styles in different ways, as we have noted, they have proposed a variety of systems that use labels that may differ considerably. The resulting plethora of terms can seem quite confusing to instructors without sufficient experience in this area of pedagogy and andragogy.

Because of the multiplicity of theories, instructors may feel tempted to completely dismiss the topic of learning styles. After all, if researchers cannot agree on the fundamentals of learning styles, and if only education specialists can devote the time and energy to make sense out of all the theories proposed, how can instructors hope to understand enough about learning styles to help their students?

That's a good question! But what seems clear in all this confusion is that whatever systems and labels might be proposed, students have individual learning needs, learn in different ways, and process information differently. For these reasons, postsecondary instructors need to give attention to learning styles.

Identifying Learning Styles

As we discussed in Chapters 1 and 2, there are dozens of ways to understand the individual learning processes of your students. The auditory/visual/tactile approach seems the simplest and most practical, for the reasons outlined in Chapter 1.

Whatever approach you choose, the first step, as previously stated, is to identify how your students learn.

How You Can Identify Learning Styles

The first step in understanding postsecondary students is to do a preliminary analysis of their learning styles. We must underscore here that such an analysis is just a beginning. Nothing at this early stage of assessing learning styles can be considered definitive.

An instructor may gain some understanding of the learning styles of his or her students through brief, personal interviews with them and discussions about how they remember simple things in their lives. This approach is similar to the exercise described in Chapter 1 and recommended for instructors.

Another simple way to help identify learning styles is through formal observation of specific behaviors. An instructor may observe students while they are completing a task and record exactly how each student approaches the task. For example, Student A might use a picture or point-by-point referencing, considering specific pieces of information in order to arrive at an understanding of the whole concept. These behaviors indicate a certain learning style, one that is holistic and perhaps visual by nature. Instructors should take note of this strategy that has been implemented so to replicate it during course implementation. Further, Student B might conceptualize the task, and Student C might appear to be using a running commentary. Each approach reveals something about how that student learns. The behaviors of both Student B and Student C indicate learning style preferences. Student B's choice of organizing and understanding information could again be holistic and indicate a visual or tactile preference. Student C's choice of a running commentary specifically points to an auditory preference for learning.

An instructor could also begin to identify learning styles through an analysis of products and processes of student learning. Analysis of products will give instructors information needed to understand individual student learning styles. Products or projects that are specific and detailed oriented give information about a student's learning style. The type of student who prefers to communicate through specific details might have an auditory bent. Also, a student who chooses to communicate information through charts, pictures, and graphs may be exhibiting a visual bent toward the learning process. By observing students as they learn and interact with the learning process, the instructor will be able to determine, for example, if a student has understood a concept in pieces or as a whole. Understanding this about a student gives many clues as to which learning style is their preference. From there instructors can continue to vary their planning and implementation of course content to assure that all learning styles are being accommodated.

How You Can Help Your Students Identify Their Learning Styles

The second step in working with learning styles is to help your students understand how they learn best. This step may be easier than some instructors might expect because of the nature of postsecondary learners and their maturity, emotional and personal as well as academic (Guild and Garger 1985). Today more than ever Guild and Garger's perspective on postsecondary learners is still valid. Postsecondary students know that the cost of their education is enormous, and that the value of the education has never meant more than it does today. For these reasons, the majority of postsecondary students are conscious of what their learning needs are and what learning environment they need to succeed.

Guild and Garger (1985) suggest some simple tools and techniques that instructors can use to help their students identify their learning styles: inventories that include preferred teaching strategies, interviews, observation, analyses of the products of learning that result from different teaching strategies, checklists, and simply having each student describe how he or she learns.

Whichever methods you use to help your students understand how they learn, you should try to keep it brief and simple so as not to detract from the goals and objectives of the class or group setting. Understanding about learning styles is a means, not an end in itself.

Also, however you choose to help your students better understand how they learn, they should assume responsibility for that effort. As they try to identify their styles, they should especially examine their styles within the context of their learning experiences and the extent to which certain strategies and approaches have succeeded or failed.

How to Accommodate Learning Styles

When you and each of your students understand how each student learns best, you should use that knowledge in planning and implementing learning experiences. As previously advocated, this venture is a responsibility shared by you and your students.

Chapters 4, 5, and 6 of this book are meant to guide you in choosing strategies and activities to better accommodate your students in terms of one approach to learning styles: auditory, visual, and tactile/kinesthetic. However, as we have mentioned, the suggestions in these chapters are related to other systems of learning styles as well.

How to Help Your Students Develop Other Styles

If the ultimate goal that you set for yourself is to help your students learn the course content more effectively, then it would be enough to accommodate their individual learning strengths. But, as we have urged, instructors must help their students expand their scope of learning.

Although each student may learn best in a certain way, he or she should also be exposed to a variety of learning experiences to become a more versatile learner and to better prepare for the real world. The next three chapters provide some ideas for building a holistic learning environment.

Understanding Your Students: Ongoing Process, Outgoing Process

Instructors should continue to observe each student throughout the semester in order to always have the most complete picture of how he or she learns, and then modify their strategies whenever necessary. As Cahn (1978) states, specific information gathered about student learning styles can be used in planning. If two or more instructors have the same student in their classes, they need to communicate information about that student and about strategies that have helped him or her succeed. They also need to dedicate professional development time to sharing successful teaching methodologies.

In some settings, this may result in several sections of a course covering the same content through different methodologies, to accommodate the learning styles of the specific students in each section. A format of this sort requires dedicated planning, a commitment to open communication, and continual attention to the individual needs and success of all students.

Conclusion

Whatever the systems for understanding how people learn, and whatever the labels used, there are similarities that can help us better understand our students, their strengths, their weaknesses, their needs, and help them learn more effectively and more holistically.

The primary purpose for understanding the different approaches to learning processes is to better appreciate the complexity of the processes and to realize the diversity of perspectives. But the myriad of labels should not cause us to become bewildered or fixated; we need to remember that even though students may differ in their learning styles, they may very well have similar needs. One of the most important obligations of an effective instructor is to understand those needs.

Knowing how our students learn, we should plan learning experiences that accommodate their individual styles and that address their individual needs. We should also plan and implement intentional strategies that will empower all of our students to take control over their learning experiences. By planning classroom experiences that allow students to organize information in different ways, students of different learning styles can learn the new information. Providing outlines, charts, graphs, as well as point-by-point analysis of new information or data, the instructor has assisted with the learning process for a variety of learners. Being able to take control over learning experiences allows each student to learn from his or her individual perspective. If students are empowered in a learning situation, they will be motivated to understand and to learn the new knowledge.

These students will not feel overwhelmed by new information; they will feel as if they can handle whatever the learning experience presents. Students who feel in control of a learning situation will have a positive attitude and a positive approach. Therefore, it is critical that we understand the importance of addressing the individual learning needs of our students and of planning experiences to address those needs.

The following three chapters address the needs of the auditory learner, the visual learner, and the tactile/kinesthetic learner, respectively. In each, we also make connections between the auditory, visual, and tactile/kinesthetic system and the various other systems of learning styles.

Each chapter also includes, for the targeted type of learner, suggestions for preinstructional strategies, teaching strategies, and assessment and evaluation strategies, with specific examples for using the strategies.

The term preinstructional strategies refers to activities that prepare students for specific instructional activities and set the stage for the learning experience.

Preinstructional teaching strategies serve an important purpose. They motivate the students for the lesson and provide an opportunity for students to focus on the goals and objectives to be highlighted during the lesson. Additionally, preinstructional strategies allow the time for instructors to give students a type of road map, indicating how the lesson will progress, what the instructor and students will be working toward, and what the ultimate outcome will be.

The preinstructional time in any lesson or activity is critical for setting the tone for the lesson or activity. Therefore, it is important for instructors to use strategies here that encourage motivation and interest and that allow the students to understand and anticipate the lesson or activity to come.

Preinstructional strategies are a good idea, no matter how you teach. But they are particularly useful if you try to orient your instructional activities toward the learning styles of your students. They provide one additional and important way to help your students learn more successfully.

Most of Chapters 4, 5, and 6 are devoted to teaching strategies, with examples for using those strategies. This constitutes the heart of each of these three chapters.

However, we also consider ways of assessing and evaluating students. Assessment and evaluation are important components of the planning and organization process for any instructor. An instructor who is concerned about individual learning styles, the success of every student, and arranging the learning environment to be most positive and to promote success must necessarily consider the variety of choices for assessment and evaluation.

Instructors should keep in mind that assessment and evaluation should be both formative, or ongoing, and summative, used to judge competency.

Formative assessment and evaluation involves each and every lesson or activity, analyzing student reactions to tasks or objectives as well as student performance, interactions, and feedback. Being cognizant of how students react helps the instructor plan future lessons or activities more appropriately and better meets the learning needs of individual students.

In planning for summative evaluation, instructors must consider their students' learning styles. Just as they should plan and implement lessons or activities to make the most of learning strengths, they should design evaluation instruments in a manner that highlights those strengths. Only then will evaluation give a true picture of how well students have understood and retained information and mastered skills and how well they apply that information and those skills.

When designing instruments that are authentic, that genuinely measures student learning, it is important for instructors to remember that they may need to modify the instruments for individual students. As we have stressed, learners with certain strengths and needs—auditory, visual, or tactile—are not all alike. Instructors may need to change the time allowed to complete a certain test or change the number of items an individual student has to complete in order for the instrument to be valid. These modifications to accommodate for individual learning needs provide for a more genuine assessment of the student.

Genuine assessment gives the instructor the information necessary to continue planning and implementing lessons and activities appropriately and adequately. Genuine and authentic assessment provides better evidence that the students understand information and are prepared to continue. It is important that students understand how all information is connected and related to the real world. Then, they will be ready to acquire new information and skills. Therefore, proper, authentic, and genuine assessment is critical to ensuring a successful and positive learning situation.

Organizing both formative and summative evaluation tools within these general parameters will make the assessment authentic. Instructors will, therefore, get an accurate indication of both the present status of student learning and the level of mastery.

Reminder

As we conclude this chapter on postsecondary students and their learning styles and turn to focus on auditory, visual, and tactile styles, we should emphasize that our use of the terms auditory learner, visual learner, and tactile/kinesthetic learner is not categorical. These terms are just convenient ways to refer to learners with certain strengths or natural predominant tendencies.

Most people have combinations of these strengths or tendencies. So, when instructors accommodate students who have predominantly auditory or visual or tactile needs, they are also helping students with secondary auditory, visual, or tactile strengths and needs.

We should always bear in mind that, no matter what labels we use to help us better understand learning processes, our students are individuals. Although we may categorize learning styles according to three tendencies, we recognize and stress that each student is unique.

We cannot emphasize enough the importance of understanding students as individual learners, with individual learning styles and needs. All students need to experience success in every learning situation. These points are at the core of every instructor's professional responsibility.

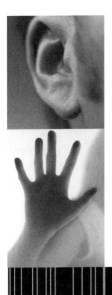

Auditory Learners

CHAPTER FOUR

T his chapter focuses on the specific characteristics of auditory learners. It suggests
preinstructional strategies that help motivate and focus auditory learners and teaching
strategies that accommodate their strengths and
needs.

We also describe strategies that postsecondary
instructors have used successfully and how instructors can modify their strategies. Then we describe
assessment and evaluation in terms of accommodating auditory learners.

Characteristics of Auditory Learners

This auditory learning style can be compared to
other labels used by researchers. Some labels for
students who are similar in learning characteristics to the auditory learner are the independent

learner, the learner who is competitive and achievement-oriented, the learner who has the ability to analyze pieces of information, and the perceptual student, who needs to understand relationships and connections between concepts and pieces of information. Auditory learners focus on the task or objective at hand. They tend to be more conceptual by nature, concerned with how concepts relate to pieces of information. They are very skill-oriented. They also memorize well.

Learners with auditory strengths tend to fall somewhere in the quadrant 2 or 3 range of the McCarthy (1987) 4MAT System for identifying learner needs. These quadrants represent abstract thinking and conceptualization skills; simply stated, these quadrants are the Thinking quadrants (McCarthy 1987).

The characteristics of auditory learners are similar to the Concrete Sequential or Abstract Sequential learner designations used by Gregorc (1985) and to the Abstract/Reflective learner as defined by Harb, Durrant, and Terry (1993) in terms of being perceptual and conceptual. Auditory learners are independent learners (Keefe and Thompson 1987), and they are field-independent and competitive (Wooldridge 1988).

The previous characteristics and the descriptors in Chart 3 should guide you in identifying students with auditory learning strengths and needs.

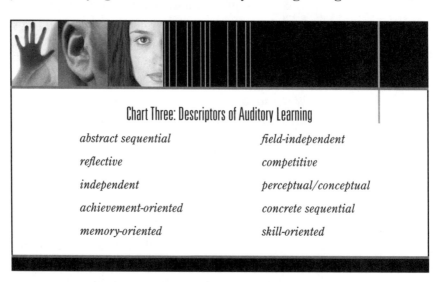

Chart Three: Descriptors of Auditory Learning

abstract sequential	field-independent
reflective	competitive
independent	perceptual/conceptual
achievement-oriented	concrete sequential
memory-oriented	skill-oriented

It should be noted at this point that schools have traditionally tended to reward the students with auditory learning strengths. Therefore, many of the teaching strategies used in today's classrooms are appropriate for the learner who prefers to learn through the auditory mode and who has experienced success with that strategy.

Preinstructional Strategies for Auditory Learners

One preinstructional teaching strategy for addressing the learning needs of the auditory learner is verbal questioning or verbal focusing. This verbal consideration of the goals, objectives, or content of the upcoming lesson or activity helps students anticipate what will be happening. Asking questions and providing a focus orally is an appropriate way to engage students who learn best in an auditory setting.

Another preinstructional teaching strategy is verbal sharing or interactions. Asking students for oral responses to questions such as, "What do you think we are going to do with these materials?" or, "What steps do you think we need to take to solve this problem?" will more fully engage the auditory learner. Not only does the oral approach appeal to the auditory preference, but questions of this type recognize that auditory learners process information sequentially and focus on the individual pieces, rather than holistically.

Also effective for the auditory learner are preinstructional teaching strategies that include a verbal rewording of directions, expectations, and important points of the upcoming lesson.

Auditory learners can answer focusing or directive questions that call for one specific answer. Using this type of question during preinstructional time will enable those students to focus on one aspect of the upcoming lesson at a time. Auditory learners memorize well and can answer such questions appropriately. As a result, they will experience success and a feeling of control over the learning situation.

Also, because auditory learners concentrate on goals and objectives, questions that focus them on the specifics of these goals and objectives constitute one of the most successful preinstructional strategies.

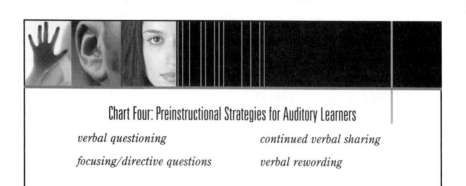

Chart Four: Preinstructional Strategies for Auditory Learners

verbal questioning   *continued verbal sharing*

focusing/directive questions   *verbal rewording*

Teaching Strategies Appropriate for Auditory Learners

The most appropriate teaching strategies for students who learn best through the auditory mode are oral. These strategies include lecture, discussion, independent work, objective presentation and practice, questioning techniques or tasks that require exact or specific answers, activities that involve memory, and verbal sorting.

Lecture

The lecture is the most commonly used of these strategies. The lecture delivers information orally in an orderly, sequential manner, so it works well for the auditory learner, who as we have noted prefers approaches that are aural, focuses on the individual pieces, and processes information sequentially.

Sometimes this lecture can be interactive, allowing for feedback from student to instructor, instructor to student, or even student to student. The interaction is generally oral, and students and instructors process information orally.

Because the lecture is the most common teaching strategy at the post-secondary level, students who learn best through the auditory mode tend to be the most successful. A teaching strategy repertoire consisting of only the lecture will therefore tend to disadvantage students who have different learning strengths.

Discussion

Discussion is a teaching strategy that also accommodates auditory students, as it allows students to acquire and process information through oral interaction. Discussions can be organized in various ways, depending upon the size of the group of students. They can involve the entire group or work with smaller groups.

Discussion can also take the form of a personal conference or interview with each individual student. This type of interaction makes the discussion similar in format to the interactive lecture. The basic difference between the two strategies is that the interactive lecture has as its goal the dissemination of specific information, while the discussion focuses in part on the opinions and perspectives of the participants. Those opinions and perspectives influence the direction, dynamics, and content of the discussion.

This aspect makes the discussion a bit different from the interactive lecture. Discussion allows students with auditory strengths to experience success because the information is treated orally.

Independent Work

Independent work is often effective with auditory students. Independent work of any kind gives them the opportunity to hear oral directions and get information orally and then complete a task appropriately. Often students with auditory strengths experience success with independent work of any kind.

Auditory students listen to a running commentary within their heads; this running commentary allows them to progress successfully through the steps of a specific task or activity. Students with auditory strengths often prefer to be told information or requirements or expectations and then be allowed to complete the task on their own. These students will continually articulate the information to themselves in order to process it and successfully complete the task.

Because auditory students are often competitive, working alone allows them the chance to progress at their own rate, as quickly as they may want (Wooldridge 1988). Also, this competitive nature and the independent organization of a lesson or task will give them the chance to process the information as they are most comfortable: orally, by running an independent commentary in their heads. Auditory learners need the opportunity to repeatedly articulate information as they complete a task. It is also not uncommon for these students to rephrase information to the instructor in order to better understand it.

Objective Presentation and Practice

Another teaching strategy and an organizational method to accommodate auditory learners is the objective presentation and practice of new information. Objective presentation of new information allows auditory learners the chance to focus on specific, individual facts, then eventually progress to learning total concepts from these individual facts. They need to feel comfortable with individual pieces of information before they can feel comfortable with a concept.

An appropriate strategy for auditory learners is programmed instruction. Information is presented systematically, one piece at a time; only after all the information has been presented is the whole concept considered. This strategy is appropriate for students who learn from the bottom up and need all the pieces to understand the whole.

Tasks that are objective and precise in format give auditory learners practice with individual pieces of new information (Butler 1988). To allow practice with specific pieces of information, an instructor can give worksheets with one piece of information practiced a number of times or worksheets with true-and-false questions or multiple-choice questions. This sort of activity is effective with auditory students.

It is critical, however, that the information first be presented orally, then later practiced in the objective form. Oral presentation of new information works well with practicing this information in some type of objective format. Again, during the objective task, the auditory student may engage in a running oral commentary to review and master the presented material.

This type of learner will succeed best at tasks that call for specific solutions. Activities that involve precise directions, such as would be used for computer or computer-aided tasks, are additional examples of the types of strategies that best accommodate auditory students.

Questions that Require Exact Answers

Auditory learners respond best to questions that require exact or specific answers. These questions are similar to objective-type tasks in that they require students to concentrate on exact or specific answers, rather than open-ended responses. Because auditory learners tend to search for a single answer or a single solution to a task or problem, they are less successful with questions that have no specific answer or may have several correct answers.

Ideally, instructors should ask questions that require only one specific answer, and they should ask them orally. In this way, they doubly accommodate auditory learners.

Activities that Involve Memory

Auditory learners tend to be successful at memorization. Because they approach learning situations step by step and piece by piece, they do well on memory work or drill work. Drills that involve committing individual pieces of information to memory are appropriate for auditory learners. Using memorization or drills is similar to the running commentary within the student's head. Just as the running commentary continually reviews new information to verify that the correct pieces are being learned, memorization allows the auditory learner the opportunity to commit to memory specific pieces of information.

Lessons or activities that involve drill and memory exercises also prepare the student to commit to long-term memory information that is necessary for future use. Information committed to long-term memory can be used as the foundation for learning new concepts.

Verbal Sorting

Verbal sorting is another teaching strategy that accommodates auditory learners (Sealey 1985). Similar to the mental running commentary, verbal sorting gives the auditory learner the opportunity to organize pieces of information into related areas by repeating or restating or orally listing new information in order to place pieces of information into related areas and eventually form larger concepts. Learning situations that involve verbal sorting accommodate the oral strengths of auditory learners and improve their chances of success.

General Advice on Accommodating Auditory Learners

It is important to underscore here that to successfully address the learning needs of their auditory learners, instructors should emphasize the oral mode as much as possible. This includes giving directions orally and allowing students to give presentations orally, orally engaging in feedback with instructors, and restating and memorizing new information.

If students with auditory strengths are allowed to present orally, the instructor may assess more accurately exactly what information the students have processed and understood and the areas in which they need further work. This knowledge can then influence future planning and instructional strategies.

To further accommodate the auditory learner, tasks and activities should be as ordered and sequential as possible. Because this type of learner learns information best in pieces, those pieces should be presented in an orderly fashion, in a logical sequence. Auditory learners need to understand natural relationships among the things that they are learning, so the pieces of new information should be arranged in a way that interrelates them.

Auditory learners process information deliberately and methodically (Gregorc 1985). They learn information in its most literal sense. They understand information as it is presented on the surface, not attempting to find subliminal meanings or relationships. For these reasons, it is important for instructors to plan and organize lessons and activities as precisely and exactly as possible, with no hidden meanings or objectives. Otherwise, auditory learners will become frustrated and their motivation may suffer. This lack of interest may lead them to participate less, which could make them seem poorly prepared, not conscientious, or unable to master new information.

Because auditory learners are precise, logical, and definite, they also prefer to interact with information that is concrete, if at all possible. When information is presented, it is important for them to be able to use that information. For example, they can better understand the relationship of supply and demand through a concrete example, such as concert tickets that are in high demand, and they better understand the steps of the judicial process if they actually participate in a case on their campus.

Further, it is also possible to engage auditory learners in analyzing information once they have had ample opportunity to interact with it and have mastered it. Auditory learners will succeed at such tasks if they are allowed to do the analysis orally, or independently, or by using their mental running commentary as a substitute for speaking out loud.

Because some auditory learners are competitive by nature, some are also product-oriented. They are concerned with finishing a task and having a concrete result. However, it is important to underscore again that, before they begin the task, the information must first be presented precisely and logically, and the expectations for completing the task must also be sequential and ordered.

Auditory learners process information after they have heard it or after engaging in a running commentary. It is critical to allow auditory learners *thinking time*. This time is often called *wait time*. Although thinking time and wait time have similar characteristics, they are different and must be considered independently of one another when referring to the auditory learner. The auditory learner needs the thinking time. The thinking time allows the student to specifically highlight points of information or data in their head. The thinking time may also be used to re-auditorize information or data in an oral way that is best for auditory students to learn new concepts and/or information.

Wait time can also be used to order and highlights points, but sometimes it is just used to formulate an answer. Again, wait time and thinking time can be similar, depending on how a student uses it. Instructors need to be aware and understand the different ways students may use this time. This understanding leads to certain expectations and certain strategies during the teaching process.

Wait time is related to thinking time or processing time in that it is the time an instructor allows students to think about an appropriate response to a question. Wait time should allow auditory learners ample opportunity to hear the question, process it, process an answer, and give that answer.

Thinking time or processing time, in general, is the time that students need to process any information given in a learning situation. In organizing a lesson, it is critical to plan for thinking time or processing time, because auditory learners need to first hear information and then have the time to process it.

Many instructors find it easier to allow wait time because there is a definite result: the answer. It is more difficult for instructors to allow for thinking time or processing time because the process is open ended: instructors often do not know exactly when auditory learners have processed something.

It is helpful then to include other oral strategies: such as feedback, restating by both instructor and students, and paraphrasing to ensure adequate processing time. Many instructors find that auditory learners are the most difficult to read through body language in a learning situation. Auditory learners may appear to be unfocused, when in reality they may be processing information, using a running commentary to review information, or attempting to link new information logically to information already learned. Therefore, it is important for instructors to use responses as indicators of their students' levels of understanding. Many times auditory learners do not ask for rephrasing of information. It is crucial for instructors to understand that many times students do not understand their learning style completely. Therefore, they are unable to ask for the teaching strategy to best facilitate their learning. These auditory learners may indeed need oral rephrasing of information in order to comprehend then information and then be able to use it. Instructors need to be aware that rephrasing is an important component of the auditory learning style and consistently build rephrasing into lessons and activities. As referred to previously in this text, providing various teaching strategies throughout a course and/or unit ensures that different learning styles are addressed.

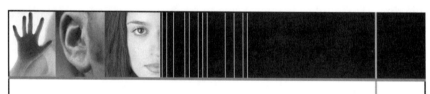

Chart Five: Teaching Strategies for Auditory Learners

lecture	tasks with specific answers
oral directions	memorization/memory work
discussion	verbal sorting
independent tasks	sequential presentation
objective presentation and practice	thinking time
programmed instruction	

Student Reactions: What Do They Reveal?

In order to appropriately accommodate learners with auditory strengths and needs, we should be aware of how those students react to learning situations. Those reactions may indicate certain, specific learning needs, which we should keep in mind as we plan and implement lessons or activities.

A common reaction of auditory learners is to ask the instructor to repeat directions, expectations, and new information. This type of reaction indicates that these auditory learners could not process adequately what the instructor said and that they may need to hear it again, possibly rephrased. An instructor should respond positively to such requests because the amount of time auditory learners need to process oral information may vary greatly. This is an important point for instructors to remember when planning lessons or activities to accommodate auditory styles.

Another typical reaction of auditory learners is to ask for additional information to be provided in order to clearly understand a topic or a task. When an instructor plans lessons or activities, it is important to keep in mind that it may often be necessary to expand upon topics beyond the scope of initial planning to give students greater exposure to new information and more examples. Some auditory learners may need that exposure and those examples to fully process and comprehend the pieces of new information that they are learning.

The instructor who pays careful attention to student reactions in a classroom or group setting gains insight into the thinking process of auditory learners. Adjusting the lesson focus or objectives to accommodate the needs of auditory learners will make the learning situation more positive and the experience more successful.

Again, we must stress that the term auditory learner simply refers to students with auditory strengths and needs. We must always acknowledge and remember that there are considerable differences among those students. Instructors should pay particular attention to the differences among student reactions to a lesson or activity or during classroom or group interaction in general.

For example, reactions to oral directions may be generally positive among the auditory learners, but individual students may also need an opportunity to outline and/or list the same information in order to assist with processing the information. This sometimes is referred to as a formal lecture with programmed notes (Harb, Durrant, and Terry 1993).

Another student whose preferential learning style is auditory may also need to have a formal lecture and some type of demonstration to accompany the lecture. This auditory learner has secondary learning needs that touch upon the visual learning style.

Still another example would be an auditory learner who needs the instructor or other students to model the approach to a specific task. That need might reveal some secondary learning preferences in the visual mode.

Finally, an auditory learner may also have secondary tactile or kinesthetic learning preferences. This student may need oral directions and oral information but then also the opportunity to interact hands on with the information, such as in an experiment.

All of these examples show how important it is for us to always have a sense of how our students may be reacting to the ways in which new information is presented, as well as how they approach learning situations. Students who have had the chance to learn about how they naturally prefer to approach learning situations will most likely be able to articulate clearly what else they might need in a learning situation in order to succeed. However, many students just may not know what they need; to better understand the needs of these students, then, we must be sensitive to their reactions to a lesson or an activity.

For example, it is not enough to respond to the student who clearly states that an outline would be a helpful addition to the formal lecture. It is important also to read the reactions of other students, such as the student who is not willingly answering questions or the student who asks questions that require the instructor to restate information in various ways. If students continually ask for rephrasing of information during a presentation, it is safe to assume that they are not adequately understanding the information as it is presented orally. The instructor should then use strategies to supplement the oral presentation.

It is important to underscore here that the primary way to accommodate the learning needs of auditory learners is to present new information orally. However, to ensure that these auditory learners fully understand

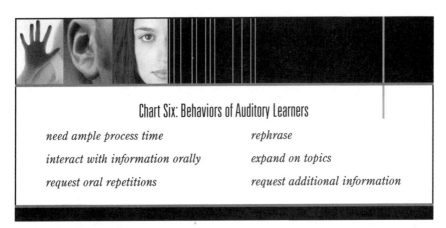

Chart Six: Behaviors of Auditory Learners

need ample process time

interact with information orally

request oral repetitions

rephrase

expand on topics

request additional information

that information, the instructor must also consider their secondary learning preferences.

Assessment and Evaluation of Auditory Learners

Objective, specific questions will give instructors the needed information regarding the learning process for individual auditory learners. These questions can be asked orally and informally to assess what students have learned from an individual lesson or activity. The questions can also be in a written format, in the form of objective questions such as multiple-choice, true-false, fill-ins, or short answers.

If these written, objective questions are used as formative assessment, they often are not graded. The instructor uses the information gained from them to modify lesson plans to meet the needs of individual learners and/or to generally plan for future lessons.

Summative evaluation that addresses the style of auditory learners and genuinely assesses what they have learned is very specific. To address auditory learning strengths, instruments should include some specific types of questions and should be designed in a specific format.

Examples of specific types of questions that could be included in a formal test to accommodate the auditory learning style are objective questions such as multiple-choice, true-false, matching, and fill-ins. These types of questions are consistent with the auditory learner's preferential learning style in that they are definitive, they have one precise answer, and they require individual, specific pieces of information. Summative evaluation using such questions will give a genuine picture of the knowledge that students have mastered because auditory learners tend to learn information one piece at a time.

Another example of a summative evaluation instrument would be an independent research project that requires research and reporting on a topic that is precise or specific. This project allows auditory learners, who tend to be independent by nature, the opportunity to apply pieces of information that they have learned to an expanded topic or issue, at their own pace, in their own time and format. Because of their independent style, auditory learners will respond well to a project of this type.

Still another example of summative evaluation to accommodate auditory learners is to have them share with the instructor information that they have memorized. Therefore, they would prefer oral tests and reports that require them to repeat orally new information that is important to understand, memorize, or master.

Conclusion

We need to acknowledge and remember that auditory learners have individual and specific learning needs. In planning to accommodate the auditory learning style, we need to understand and keep in mind their specific needs.

Auditory learners must be presented with materials and tasks orally, whenever possible. In addition, it is important to remember that some of these students may also have secondary learning needs. Often these secondary needs require visual or tactile experiences to supplement the auditory experiences. For such students, a combination of approaches might be critical to success in the learning situation, from planning through evaluation.

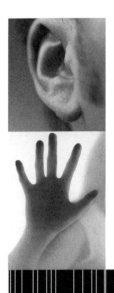

Visual
Learners

CHAPTER FIVE

T his chapter focuses on the specific characteristics of visual learners. It suggests pre-instructional strategies that help motivate and focus visual learners and teaching strategies that accommodate their strengths and needs.

We also describe strategies that postsecondary instructors have used successfully and how instructors can modify their strategies. Then, we describe assessment and evaluation in terms of accommodating visual learners.

Characteristics of Visual Learners

Because many schools tend to favor auditory learners, visual learners may experience difficulty in learning situations. Visual learners who cannot learn in any other mode are in a sense completely the opposite of auditory learners: these students get nothing from merely hearing information.

Visual learners need to interact visually with new information. Research has given these learners labels such as global, affective, dependent, concept-oriented, field-sensitive, field-dependent, and abstract random or concrete random (Butler 1988). These students tend to perceive the whole of a concept, rather than just its individual parts. Visual learners are generally group oriented, they respond well to environmental influences or social cues, and they work better in informal rather than formal learning situations.

According to McCarthy (1987) and her 4MAT System for identifying learners and their needs, students with visual strengths or preferences tend to fall somewhere in the quadrant 1 or 4 range. These quadrants represent concrete experience skills; simply stated, such students tend to sense and feel (McCarthy 1987).

The characteristics of visual learners are similar to the abstract random learner designations used by Gregorc (1985), because abstract random learners learn holistically, taking in information from multiple areas in order to understand a new concept.

The visual style can be related to the concrete learner (Harb, Durrant, and Terry 1993) and perhaps also to the active learner.

Visual learners have many of the same characteristics as field-sensitive and field-dependent learners (Anderson 1995). These characteristics include showing interest in the world around them, being emotional, using nonverbal cues in addition to words, and identifying with values and feelings to understand a situation as a whole.

Visual learners can also be considered as dependent learners (Keefe and Thompson 1987). Dependent learners perceive the whole before they perceive or attempt to understand the parts of the whole. They are global learners: they depend on the environment for learning cues or clues.

Wooldridge (1988) considers learners with attributes similar to those of visual, field-sensitive, and dependent learners to have an affective learning style. This style is characterized by a holistic focus. Such learners pay attention to complete aspects of concepts and learning situations. Emotions, values, and outside stimuli play an important role in their learning.

The characteristics listed previously and the descriptors in Chart 7 should guide you in identifying students with visual learning strengths and needs.

It is important to remember at this preliminary point that learning situations for postsecondary learners most commonly favor auditory learners and disadvantage visual learners. Therefore, to accommodate students with visual learning strengths and needs, instructors need to almost completely abandon conventional approaches and develop innovative ways to address the learning needs of visual learners.

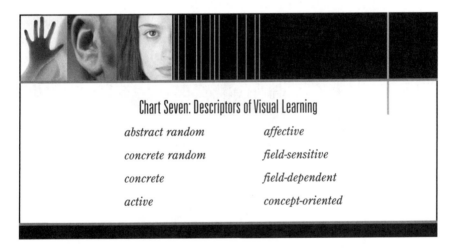

Chart Seven: Descriptors of Visual Learning

abstract random	*affective*
concrete random	*field-sensitive*
concrete	*field-dependent*
active	*concept-oriented*

Preinstructional Strategies for Visual Learners

One preinstructional strategy that targets the needs of visual learners is focusing in writing. Instructors may write the goals or objectives of the upcoming lesson or activity either on the board or in the form of a visual guide or outline.

Another preinstructional strategy would be to give students focusing questions in writing, again either on the board or on paper. The purpose of these focusing questions is to allow the students to interact visually with the main intent of the upcoming lesson or activity. If prepared appropriately, these questions will engage students in thinking critically about the concepts, issues, and information to be presented in the lesson or activity. For visual learners, it is critical that these questions be provided in some sort of visual format.

Because visual students tend to be holistic in their approach to learning, they will benefit from preinstructional strategies that expose them to the whole concept or issue to be addressed. Visual stimuli may include a picture of the whole concept, a short written description of the concept, or merely a short group of written words stating exactly what will follow. If materials for an upcoming lesson or activity seem to be appropriate for oral introduction only, the instructor should attempt to provide visual alternatives, such as providing directions through photos or pictures rather than verbally alone.

Preliminary instructions or focusing questions, goals, or objectives can also be presented through diagrams or charts. This format will allow visual learners an opportunity to process the preliminary information about the lesson in a mode with which they are most comfortable.

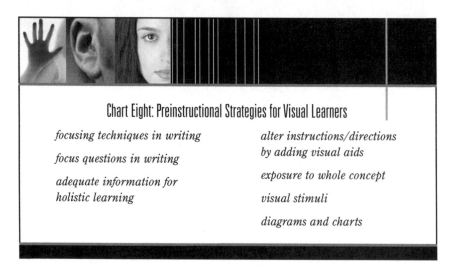

Chart Eight: Preinstructional Strategies for Visual Learners

focusing techniques in writing

focus questions in writing

adequate information for holistic learning

alter instructions/directions by adding visual aids

exposure to whole concept

visual stimuli

diagrams and charts

Teaching Strategies Appropriate for Visual Learners

The most appropriate teaching strategies for students who learn best through the visual mode must, of course, include visual formats. Instructors should also consider using social cues, small groups, graphic organizers, models, and demonstrations, role-playing, student presentations, field trips, motivational accounts or stories, computer-aided instruction, webbing, and activities that allow freedom and emphasize creativity.

Visual Formats

Instructors can put materials to be learned on bulletin boards, in graphic forms, or in diagrams and charts. Environmental conditions are important for visual learners. If such types of visual stimuli are provided as part of the environment, visual learners will be able to use them to better process the new information. Instructors can also provide opportunities for students to work in visual formats, such as with charts and diagrams.

Because visual learners are dependent, field-sensitive, and field-dependent, they rely heavily on their senses. It is important for instructors to plan lessons or activities to include stimuli that address as many senses as possible, to help visual learners understand and process new concepts and information more easily.

Social Cues

It is important for visual learners to have social cues: group interactions among students concerning a concept. Instructors can plan for including such interactions in various ways, depending on the material and the class being implemented.

Group Learning

Visual learners tend to favor a more informal setting. Because of this preference, they respond well when the class is organized into small, interactive groups. Small groups engaged in cooperative learning activities address the learning needs of visual learners because of their informal nature and because of their social nature. This classroom arrangement also appeals to the group orientation of visual learners, who tend to be social and can process new information by experiencing it through other people.

The instructor must plan group exercises carefully. The planning should include determining which students will form each group. Should the instructor consciously organize groups with all visual learners, for example, or should the instructor mix learning styles? If groups are homogeneous, the members will not have the advantage of experiencing other learning styles, but they will be able to focus on using their visual strengths.

However the groups may be organized, the format structure, objectives, and tasks must be clear. Once the group is defined, then the instructor can define the roles that each group member will play.

The instructor should make sure that the objectives are clear and should allow the strategies for achieving the goals to be open ended and include formation of models, charts, diagrams, and so forth to show understanding.

As each group member carries out his or her tasks, visual learners will be able to see a variety of approaches to solving a problem, completing a task, or arriving at a decision. By allowing visual learners the opportunity to experience different ways to reach a goal or achieve an objective, the instructor is expanding their repertoire of learning strategies better than one instructor could realistically do through any one specific lesson or activity.

It is important to note that group work, cooperative learning activities, is appropriate for students of any age. However, careful planning is critical to the success of these types of strategies. Instructors need to be explicit about organization, roles, goals, and objectives, and they need to prepare and provide appropriate materials and resources, but they should leave the strategy open ended. What is positive in cooperative learning activities is that there often is no single solution to a given problem. Groups may arrive at completely different processes, students learn from each other. The task, however, remains the same: to learn a specific concept.

Cooperative learning exercises lend themselves to open-ended formats. Such formats are interactive by nature and thus of particular benefit to visual learners as well as tactile learners. Because visual learners prefer open-ended learning experiences, group work or cooperative learning exercises will allow them to experience success.

Visual learners, affective by nature (Wooldridge 1988), respond best to less-structured environments. Open-ended learning situations and open-ended teaching strategies address their learning needs most successfully.

However, because visual learners are dependent learners (Keefe and Thompson 1987), they are easily distracted. Instructors must remember this, especially in informal learning situations, such as in small group activities. Instructors might consistently monitor their visual students in such situations to help keep them on task.

Graphic Organizers

Another appropriate strategy is the use of graphic organizers, both to orient and to motivate visual learners. These might be charts, graphs, diagrams, any means of helping the students organize information visually.

Models and Demonstrations

To accommodate students with visual strengths and needs, instructors should use models and provide demonstrations whenever possible. These provide the stimuli that can help such learners more appropriately experience new materials and concepts. These demonstrations can be planned and given by the instructor, perhaps involving some of the students, or they can be researched, planned, and given by the students. Visual learners will benefit from experiencing new information or concepts in the interactive format of the demonstration.

Role-playing and Student Presentations

McCarthy (1987) states that visual learners fall into her quadrants 1 and 4. Students who fall into these quadrants need specific teaching strategies such as role-playing. Role-playing works well for visual learners in that they are able to see a new concept or new information presented in a concrete way and to experience new things interactively. This outside environmental stimulus is critical for them.

Student presentations also are effective for learners with visual strengths and needs. These presentations must involve more than just a lecture or oral dissemination of information; if organized in a multifaceted format, presentations engage visual learners and allow them to process new concepts and new information in a more holistic way. This is exactly how a visual learner must have information presented.

Field Trips

Field trips are also important for the student who learns best visually, according to McCarthy (1987). Fields trips, whether through actual visits or through virtual reality, allow visual learners to experience holistically the environment that they are learning about. If, for example, students are learning a marketing concept, visual learners will understand more completely the individual pieces of this concept once they have experienced the whole process at work.

It is important to underscore here that visual learners need to experience concepts holistically first, before they can understand or learn individual aspects or specific points of the concepts.

Motivational Accounts or Stories

Using motivational accounts or stories accompanied by visual aids, such as pictures, is also a successful teaching strategy for visual learners. Such accounts or stories that connect information or a concept to something of interest to the students not only motivate the students through relevance, but they also allow the students the opportunity to actively interact with the new information or new concept. In fact, supplementing any oral presentation of a concept with visual aids will help students with visual needs process new information and concepts.

Computer-Aided Instruction

Computer-aided instruction provides another way to reinforce the learning environment visually. Of course, the computer program must be appropriate to the concept being presented. Instructors should preview every program to validate the content and the presentation, not simply trust the promises of marketers and the lure of technology. Appropriate software, used properly, can be an effective way to accommodate visual learners.

Webbing

As previously noted, visual learners, who are very relational are linked to abstract random learners (Gregorc 1985). Teaching strategies that address this type of learner's needs include using webbing to present information or concepts. The instructor puts a concept on the board or an overhead, then encourages the students to branch off from that concept with short, specific examples or ideas. This activity allows visual learners to experience a whole concept and specific aspects of that concept in a visual format, so that they can physically see relationships and connections.

Activities that Emphasize Creativity

Visual learners respond best to questions that allow freedom for several answers, not just one correct answer, or answers in alternative forms. They also prefer open-ended questions that allow the opportunity to explore a concept holistically (Butler 1988).

Because of the open-ended nature of visual learners, they prefer using their imagination and their creativity. Lessons or activities that incorporate "What if ...?" questions and encourage individual interpretations and solutions work well with visual learners.

It should be noted that instructors must remember that visual learners may sometimes appear unfocused during a lesson or activity. They should not assume that these students lack motivation or are not attending to the task at hand. They may simply be taking time to imagine or make a concept real for themselves, making a mental picture of a new concept in order to process or understand it fully.

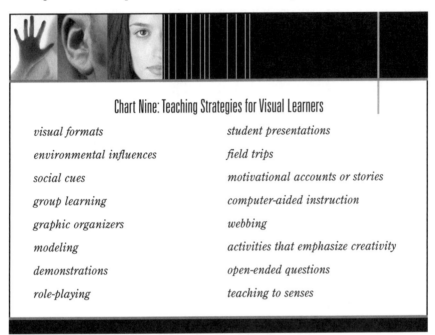

Chart Nine: Teaching Strategies for Visual Learners

visual formats	*student presentations*
environmental influences	*field trips*
social cues	*motivational accounts or stories*
group learning	*computer-aided instruction*
graphic organizers	*webbing*
modeling	*activities that emphasize creativity*
demonstrations	*open-ended questions*
role-playing	*teaching to senses*

Student Reactions: What Do they Reveal?

In order to appropriately accommodate learners with visual strengths and needs, we should be aware of how those students react to learning situations. Those reactions may indicate certain, specific learning needs, which we should keep in mind as we plan and implement lessons or activities.

As previously mentioned, visual learners may appear to not be paying attention when they are actually focused on what is happening. Their behavior may indicate only that they are taking the critical time needed to process new information or new concepts and attempt to form a mental picture. This is a particularly important reaction for instructors to note with visual learners.

Visual learners also commonly take time to either web a concept on a sheet of paper or rewrite or outline important points. Webbing a new concept gives the visual learner an opportunity to see the concept as a whole and to see how all the parts are related to this whole. In outlining new concepts, the visual learner can link different aspects of the whole concept in a way that illustrates their relationships. If a webbing activity or an outlining activity has not been planned as a specific component of a learning situation, it is important that visual learners have the time to organize the new information in these ways.

If students understand that such strategies may help them process and learn information more successfully, they may automatically use them. Instructors may want to introduce, model, and encourage these strategies so that students see the benefits.

Another common reaction of visual learners in a learning situation is to repeat new information to other students in an attempt to interact in a group situation. As stated previously, visual learners prefer informal learning situations and cooperative activities and the use of social cues. If a visual learner seems to want to engage in a group discussion, even during a formal lecture-type situation, it does not necessarily mean that he or she is being rude, is not interested in the lecture, or is not paying attention. It simply may be the natural tendency of the field-sensitive visual learner to articulate new information in a group setting in order to get other perspectives.

Visual, dependent, or field-sensitive learners show another common behavior, which is so simplistic that it may seem irrelevant. However, it is quite important.

These students may fail to show mastery of new concepts or information whether the testing situation is informal or formal, oral or written. That failure may indicate on the surface that the student has merely not prepared well enough, been attentive enough, or cared enough about learning. But the real reason may lie even deeper. It may be that the teaching strategies used to present the concepts or information did not sufficiently accommodate the visual learning style and allow the student to adequately process the material.

The instructor may be able to identify the real reason through formal observation, in-depth interviewing or conferencing with the student, or careful review of the process through which the student interacted with the new material. Then, the instructor can plan the appropriate response. If there was a problem with the presentation, the instructor can modify his or her teaching strategies to better accommodate the visual learning style.

As previously mentioned, visual learners may appear unfocused, needing time to process information to form a mental image of a concept. This behavior is especially common when the instructor does not allow adequate wait time.

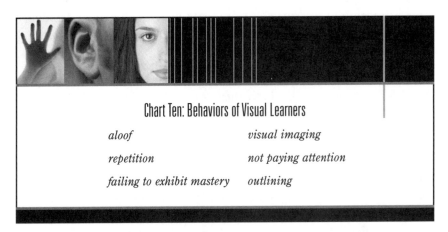

Chart Ten: Behaviors of Visual Learners

aloof	*visual imaging*
repetition	*not paying attention*
failing to exhibit mastery	*outlining*

Assessment and Evaluation of Visual Learners

Research shows that visual learners are at a distinct disadvantage in the traditional college classroom setting. They are disadvantaged by the standard objective, one-answer, specific, subject-centered tests that favor auditory learners. Students whose dominant learning style is visual need open-ended assessment or evaluation.

An appropriate example of authentic, open-ended assessment would be to assign a group a problem to solve, allowing the group to decide on the format and parameters, with the understanding that there may be several ways to solve the problem. The instructor then must assess the process as well as the product, observing and keeping notes on what happens in the groups.

Another example of open-ended assessment or evaluation that accommodates visual learners is the project. Students should be given the flexibility to use pictures, diagrams, charts, or outlines in order to show their mastery of the material in a more subjective way. To ensure that assessment and evaluation address students of all learning styles, the project approach can be combined with objective tests.

If an instructor chooses to administer objective tests, he or she should consider including essay or short-answer questions to accommodate visual learners. It might also help students to be allowed to depart from the usual narrative answer format. Visual learners may feel more comfortable answering with pictures or a web to demonstrate knowledge of the relationship of all aspects of the topic being tested. This flexibility will give such students a sense that the question is more subjective and that it can be answered more holistically.

Another positive way to more appropriately assess the knowledge of visual learners is through individual research projects and classroom presentations. Such projects and presentations give visual learners the opportunity to explore, explain, and present material in an open-ended and holistic manner with which they are comfortable.

A project such as this may lead to additional assessment and evaluation components, such as a demonstration. This format allows visual learners a holistic and graphic approach to showing mastery. Demonstrations may be particularly appropriate for the visual, dependent, field-sensitive learner if they include applying the new material, such as showing how a new process works or how new information can be used in the real world. The demonstration should include all important aspects of the material and meet the criteria the instructor has deemed necessary to show mastery.

Sims and Sims (1995a) encourage instructors to include at least one major oral assignment in their assessment. This type of assignment would ensure visual learners the opportunity to present a topic in a flexible manner with visuals.

Further, short-term assignments are sometimes successful for visual learners because they can see more immediately what they have understood and what areas need more attention. Because visual or field-dependent learners rely heavily on stimuli from the environment, the use of immediate feedback suits their learning style well.

Conclusion

We need to first acknowledge that some of our students are visual learners. The next step is to help those students understand their strengths and needs. We can do so by engaging the students in tasks that involve strengths from various learning styles, but particularly visual. We can also encourage students to describe and/or demonstrate the learning strategies that are most comfortable and most successful for them, to show their learning strengths. Then, we can plan learning situations and use strategies such as those suggested in this chapter to accommodate our visual learners.

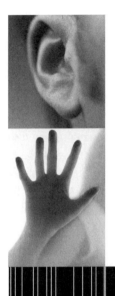

Tactile Learners

CHAPTER SIX

T his chapter focuses on the specific characteristics of tactile learners. It suggests pre-instructional strategies that help motivate and focus tactile learners and teaching strategies that accommodate their strengths and needs.

We also describe strategies that postsecondary instructors have used successfully and how instructors can modify their strategies. Then, we describe assessment and evaluation in terms of accommodating tactile learners.

Characteristics of Tactile Learners

Tactile or kinesthetic learners learn best by doing. They must be actively engaged in actually doing something in order to learn it or understand it completely.

As we have stressed, the auditory learner is the type of student most commonly rewarded in postsecondary classrooms, because most lessons are organized around lectures. The visual learner is less accommodated; sometimes instructors use the board and overhead projectors to supplement their presentations, which lessens the disadvantage for visual learners.

The tactile learning style is the most neglected at the postsecondary level. The needs of tactile learners are rarely addressed, other than in classrooms intended for actual doing, such as science laboratories. Consequently, it is critical for instructors in all academic disciplines to understand the learning characteristics of tactile learners and to address their needs.

Instructors must understand that tactile learners need opportunities for creative, hands-on learning experiences. They tend to be creative, and they need ample chance to exercise this creativity. Hands-on experiences are consistent with their need to be actively involved in the learning process.

Another characteristic of tactile learners is their need to keep moving. They need to move much more than just their fingers holding a pen. This may seem simplistic, but instructors must acknowledge this need and attempt to incorporate movement in different and creative ways.

An extremely important characteristic of tactile learners is their need to interact with the concrete as much as possible. Without concrete resources and materials, the tactile learner will not experience complete success in any learning situation.

Also of particular importance to students with tactile strengths is that the classroom or group setting be arranged appropriately. Resources and materials must be accessible for easy interaction. They must be placed within close proximity of the tactile learners so they feel that what they need is within their reach. Also, tactile learners must be able to hold, touch, and manipulate these resources and materials.

According to McCarthy (1987) and her 4MAT System for identifying learners and their needs, tactile learners fit into quadrants 3 and 4. These quadrants represent practical and proactive learners; simply stated, such students tend to learn by doing.

Unlike visual and auditory learners, tactile learners are both dependent and independent, according to the Keefe and Thompson (1987) classification. As dependent learners, they need stimuli from the environment or learning situation in order to learn successfully, while as independent learners they need to be free to interact with these stimuli on their own.

Tactile learners can be associated with concrete sequential and random learners (Butler 1988, Gregorc 1985) and with behavioral learners (Sims and Sims 1995a). They rely on sensory modes, particularly feeling (Wooldridge 1988), and they are active/concrete (Harb, Durrant, and Terry 1993).

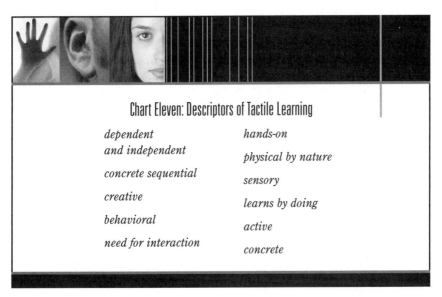

Chart Eleven: Descriptors of Tactile Learning

dependent and independent	*hands-on*
concrete sequential	*physical by nature*
creative	*sensory*
behavioral	*learns by doing*
need for interaction	*active*
	concrete

Preinstructional Strategies for Tactile Learners

Appropriate focusing techniques for tactile learners should include having available from the start the materials or resources to be used in the learning situation. This will allow tactile learners the chance to physically interact with the materials in advance of the activity. This hands-on opportunity helps tactile learners focus on the intent of the upcoming lesson and become familiar with the resources and materials that will be important in the lesson or activity to follow. Examples of having materials and resources readily available is easier in some academic areas than others. For example, the sciences appropriately lend themselves more to materials and resources such as experimental materials: items to be studied, reviewed under a microscope, and other material. It is convenient and necessary to arrange a lab in an advance of a specific experiment.

In other academic areas such as history, this method of preinteraction with materials becomes more difficult. In areas such as this it is helpful for tactile students to have pictures, artifacts, videos, and such available for them to preview and interact with. This enables the students to have an active participation in the anticipated lesson/activity.

An instructor can prepare the tactile learner for the upcoming learning experience through questioning techniques that are related to the materials or resources to be used. Because the learning strength of the tactile learner demands physical interaction of some sort, it is critical for the instructor to understand the natural link for tactile learners between focus questions and materials. Open-ended questions that allow for a variety of appropriate answers and that lead the learner to begin to probe into the new concept, combined with a chance to interact with the resources or materials, are the best type of preinstructional questions for tactile learners. Such questions as, "How might this object be affected by this other object?" or, "What do you think will happen if we mix these two ingredients together?" encourage the tactile learner to interact with the materials, begin to explore the answers, and engage in the lesson or activity.

Manipulatives in general prepare the tactile learner well for an upcoming lesson. This is true even if the materials to be manipulated are merely left in the classroom with no type of focusing techniques. Whether or not the instructor models the use of these materials, the tactile learner will naturally want to touch, hold, and interact with them. The materials in themselves provide a focus for the tactile learner, who can explore the properties of the materials and begin to understand them.

Also in preparation for the formal learning experience, an instructor may accommodate the tactile learning style by changing or supplementing the materials produced by publishers or other sources. As we have noted, postsecondary education traditionally has neglected the tactile learner, so adaptations may be needed to compensate for this neglect.

For example, a manipulative component might be added to the introduction of a concept or new information, as well as to the lesson or activity itself. Also, the materials being used may be modified to better include the tactile learner. Many of the prepared materials include strategies that address the learning needs of tactile learners only as an enrichment component, not as an integral part of the unit. Manipulative components must be incorporated into the unit, not just appended. If these components are treated only as enrichment, tactile learners may not acquire adequate command of the new concept or information to engage successfully in the enrichment activity. Therefore, it is critical for instructors to integrate into the preinstructional process, modified as appropriate, the resources and materials to be used in a lesson or activity to accommodate tactile learners.

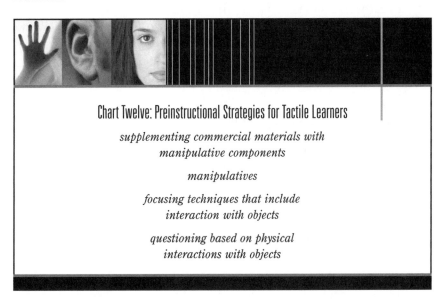

Chart Twelve: Preinstructional Strategies for Tactile Learners

supplementing commercial materials with manipulative components

manipulatives

focusing techniques that include interaction with objects

questioning based on physical interactions with objects

Teaching Strategies Appropriate for Tactile Learners

Tactile learners, like quadrant 3 and 4 learners (McCarthy 1987), learn best when they are engaged in some sort of direct contact with concepts and information through such strategies as internships and practica, field trips, experiential learning activities, simulations, and demonstrations.

Internships and Practica

Programs that incorporate internships or practicum experiences, such as in teacher education, social services, and business, address the learning needs of tactile learners by design. They provide for real experiences in which students have an extended opportunity to put into practice what they have learned in the classroom.

But we must not leave the needs of tactile learners to the internship or practicum experience. In every course, whenever possible, it is important to provide manipulative, hands-on, experiential situations.

Field Trips

A most effective way to do so is through the field trip. It puts students into a real world situation for firsthand experience with concepts and information at work. Many instructors at the postsecondary level tend not to consider field trip experiences or avoid them because they seem too complicated. However, such outings into the real world can be an invaluable means of accommodating tactile learning strengths and needs.

Experiential Learning Activities

Another way to provide experience with concepts and information at work is through experiential learning activities. Tactile learners should be provided with opportunities to "play" with components of new concepts and phenomena in an exploratory, discovery mode. Experiential learning involves doing.

For example, depending on their design and scope, laboratory experiments can constitute experiential activities. Instead of simply reading or hearing about a chemical reaction or a law of physics or a biological fact, students can create that reaction or test that law or observe that fact. This is true experiential learning at its best. The effects of such learning, experienced concretely, will become a permanent part of the tactile learner's long-term memory.

In planning such activities, we need to keep in mind that doing should involve moving the hands, the feet, both hands and feet, or the whole body. Tactile learners seem to use this movement to process new information and concepts; often they cannot adequately do so without movement. That is why tactile learners, when they are expected to process new information or concepts by just hearing them or seeing them, often feel that they are not appropriately prepared. This feeling tends to undermine their motivation.

Simulations

Because tactile learners learn best from the real thing, experiential situations should be arranged whenever possible. However, a good substitute for actual, real situations is the simulation. In a marketing class, for example, an instructor may present information about a target market for a specific product. To accommodate students with tactile strengths and needs, the instructor might show how that target marketing actually works, and then have the students plan and implement a marketing plan for a target population. By organizing a lesson in this manner, the instructor can address the learning needs of the tactile learner through the chance to interact with the concept of target marketing. Tactile students would then have the opportunity to interact with the target population about a specific product. The students can plan marketing pitches and resources needed to attract the target population to purchase a specific product.

Because tactile learners tend to look at the world in a precise, literal, ordered way, they tend to have problems with hidden or subliminal meanings. Instructors should arrange learning situations to be as specific and practical as possible. If, for example, history students are studying a situation that involves cause and effect, arranging a simulation of the period, complete with concrete materials, will allow tactile learners to experience what might have led to certain events during that period. Such learning experiences are more time consuming and difficult to prepare than a traditional lecture, but they better accommodate the strengths and needs of the tactile learner.

As previously noted, unlike visual and auditory learners, tactile learners are both dependent and independent. What does this mean?

As dependent learners, they need the stimuli from the environment or learning situation in order to learn successfully. The instructor needs to carefully arrange the learning situation, especially the resources, materials, and manipulatives, prior to a lesson or activity so tactile learners have the opportunity to explore them physically. This is the dependent nature of the tactile learner at its best.

However, the independent nature of tactile learners also requires that they be allowed to interact with these resources, materials, and manipulatives on their own. They need the freedom to explore the materials in an open-ended and unstructured manner, a way that is comfortable for them. This allows them the chance to experience the ways in which materials and resources may work and to make connections, comparisons, or contrasts.

We need to acknowledge both the dependent and independent components of the tactile learner and prepare the learning experiences with both in mind. For example, a specific learning situation may require that students use certain materials and figure out how they work best together. Having the specific materials available suits the dependent nature of tactile learners. Having time and space and freedom to experiment with these materials without structure suits their independent nature.

Technology, audio or video materials and computers, offers excellent ways to help accommodate the learning needs of tactile learners. Technology can provide the opportunity for the physical movement and interaction that they need to process new information and concepts, as well as the time and space to try to make sense of information and concepts in a nontraditional manner. It also allows tactile learners to learn at their own speed, in their own way, and with emphasis on whatever components they wish.

We must remember, however, that technology is not sufficient in itself for the tactile learner to succeed. These types of interactions should be complemented with real life, concrete experiences whenever possible.

Demonstrations

Often successful for the tactile learning style is a teaching strategy that encourages students to do and show what they are learning: the demonstration. This type of activity provides tactile learners the opportunity to manipulate resources and materials as necessary for their learning style and to organize them in ways with which they are comfortable. Demonstrations allow students with tactile strengths to exhibit the process by which they have made sense of the new concepts and information and how they have managed to synthesize them by manipulating them.

As previously noted, tactile learners tend to be practical. Engaging them as participants in demonstrations accommodates their need to learn by doing. Demonstrations also allow tactile learners opportunities for the physical movement they need to learn successfully. Although it might be necessary to introduce a concept orally, the real learning for students with tactile strengths comes through action.

There are definitely academic areas that do not lend themselves easily to adaptation to tactile learners. Such academic areas include, but are not limited to, the humanities and the some of the behavioral sciences. Even though it is difficult to vary teaching strategies in these areas, it is not impossible. Instructors can still arrange for the use of such strategies as case studies, where students actually become or assume a role. Case studies encourage group work and natural movement from place to place; as they are utilizing the information/date they are studying. Also, simulations and experiential learning can be integrated into the teaching of some behavioral sciences such as sociology or geography. Again, with these strategies, tactile learners need time to play with new concepts and new information. These concepts and information may only be in word form, but the open-ended nature of tactile learners require that students interact with materials or resources as well as concepts and information.

Chart Thirteen: Teaching Strategies for Tactile Learners

internship/practicum	*experiential learning*
field trip	*simulation*
direct contact	*demonstration*

Student Reactions: What Do they Reveal?

In order to appropriately accommodate learners with tactile strengths and needs, we should be aware of how those students react to learning situations. Those reactions may indicate certain, specific learning needs, which we should keep in mind as we plan and implement lessons or activities.

Tactile learners are commonly moving, seemingly disinterested, distracted, and not understanding what is being taught. They may appear aloof, distant. They tend not to participate willingly in a lesson or activity if it involves only or primarily hearing and/or seeing. They may virtually remove themselves from a learning situation that does not include some type of physical interaction.

Additionally, students whose learning style preference is tactile will sometimes give instructors the impression that they are not prepared or not interested in the lesson or task. Often instructors may misinterpret this reaction. They must be aware that, in such circumstances, this behavior may be indicating certain learning needs that are not being met at that particular time. It is critical that instructors understand this behavior and are able to assess a learning situation in order to adjust it to meet the needs of tactile learners.

It is important for instructors to conference with their students in order to encourage them to articulate what their learning needs might be. However, instructors must remember that some students may not know quite how to articulate their needs. Therefore, instructors should help their students identify their individual learning needs and determine exactly how they feel most comfortable and successful in a learning situation.

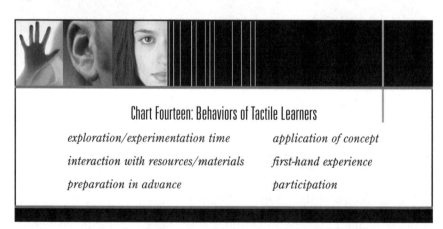

Chart Fourteen: Behaviors of Tactile Learners

exploration/experimentation time *application of concept*

interaction with resources/materials *first-hand experience*

preparation in advance *participation*

Assessment and Evaluation of Tactile Learners

The most important point for us to keep in mind when assessing or evaluating tactile learners is that we need to modify conventional strategies.

Tactile learners respond least effectively to traditional methods of testing, such as written exams or papers.

The tactile learning style demands nontraditional methods of assessment. If we do not acknowledge this fact, then we will never truly know what our students with tactile strengths have understood and can do. We will then be unable to plan appropriately for future lessons for these students. However, the important point to remember with nontraditional methods of assessment is that the criteria in the assessment must be specific and clearly identifiable as criteria necessary to be learned in a specific course. When institutions of higher education do program assessments, there are certain criteria that need to be present in each course, for each program that is being assessed. These criteria must also be shown be assessed adequately in each individual course. So, if instructors are using nontraditional methods of assessment in course, specifically assessment methods that address the tactile learner, the criteria required in the course needs to be clearly identifiable in the nontraditional assessment.

Voss (1993) clearly states that only after careful observation of a student was she able to understand that his learning style was strictly tactile. The student had been preliminarily labeled as inattentive, unmotivated, well below grade level in reading, and possibly learning-disabled. After observing, talking, and interacting with this student, Voss found that this student had mastery in areas where he had been judged deficient. All that he needed was the opportunity to demonstrate his abilities in a physical manner. By having the opportunity to put an engine back together and talk through this process very clearly, the student was to able to physically demonstrate the concepts of relationships and different things working together, and understanding of reactions of different parts of the engine, and the logic of how engine parts work together.

It is critical for us to recognize the tactile strengths and needs of our students and to know that such students cannot be adequately assessed by traditional paper-and-pencil methods or through assignments that require research and an oral presentation. Tactile learners must be assessed and evaluated in ways that address their particular learning style, especially if they have learned through physical interaction.

The primary means of assessment and evaluation appropriate for tactile learners is the demonstration. The demonstration gives the tactile learner the chance to show what he or she has learned.

Role-playing is another way to assess tactile learners appropriately, with flexibility, especially in the arts and humanities. This form of assessment accommodates for the tactile style in that it encourages active involvement in the material. Role-playing is an activity that is comfortable, enjoyable, and natural for the tactile learner, and it provides the instructor with a truer picture of what the student has learned and is able to use.

Another appropriate method for assessing tactile learners is to have them prepare a simulation, build a replica, or create an exhibit to show what they have learned.

This type of assessment can be combined with others in order to involve all learning styles at once: visual, auditory, and tactile. Allowing students to do different tasks according to their individual learning styles will give the instructor a more appropriate assessment of each student, showing more accurately what he or she has learned. An auditory learner might do written or oral work, while a visual learner might prepare graphic media to represent material in a holistic way, while a tactile learner could create models or bring in objects to show understanding. This then becomes a group assessment and evaluation tool that gives the instructor flexibility to assess students as individual learners with individual learning styles.

Conclusion

In order to adequately understand the learning needs of the tactile learner, we must consider how this type of learner best approaches a learning task. We should appreciate the importance of physical involvement for these students.

We should accept our responsibility to plan, implement, and evaluate learning situations that will provide opportunities for our students with tactile learning strengths to learn in a manner with which they are comfortable.

Tactile learners represent a minority in classroom settings, and they tend to be neglected. Instructors sometimes assume that these students can easily adapt to learning situations and strategies that favor visual or auditory learners.

But such an attitude further disadvantages tactile learners. We must carefully identify these students, understand their learning needs, and plan specifically to help them succeed.

Significance of Learning Styles Research

CHAPTER SEVEN

L earning theory has had significant implications for instructors at colleges and universi-
ties. Research shows that learners of all
ages have individual learning styles. No longer can
it be ignored that students at the postsecondary
level have learning needs that we must accommodate in order for them to make the most of their
abilities and our efforts. Instructors need to understand this learning style research and incorporate
the findings in their teaching.

How Do Your Students Learn?

We first must plan a process by which we can come
to an understanding of the learning styles of our
students and their specific needs. The plan must
include thorough observations, interviews, assistance for the students in articulating how they

approach learning tasks, and experimenting with a variety of teaching strategies. We should have our plan in place before we engage our students in learning experiences to start identifying preferences as soon as possible. As we and our students learn about how they learn, we can plan more appropriate teaching strategies to accommodate those individual strengths and needs.

Adult learning theory shows that many postsecondary students have developed strategies to cope with learning situations that were not compatible with their individual learning styles. Therefore, it may be difficult for postsecondary students to comprehend why an instructor may be interested in how they learn naturally, and why an instructor would modify his or her teaching strategies to accommodate those natural styles.

It becomes important, then, for instructors to share information with their students about learning styles and teaching strategies to accommodate those styles. As they do, students will perhaps be able to attach words or descriptors to processes that they may have been using for years. By sharing information about learning styles, instructors will be helping their students gain power and control over their personal learning styles and over their learning.

Most postsecondary students are at a point in their development when they are searching for their complete individuality in all aspects of their lives. They may be searching for a complete understanding of themselves socially, emotionally, physically, and intellectually. This holistic understanding of themselves as individuals needs to include the way in which they take in, process, and use information and the strategies that are most useful for them.

In this search, the instructor can serve as facilitator, asking the right questions, arranging the proper tasks, and engaging the students in the appropriate activities. If we assume this responsibility, our students will naturally find many of the answers to questions about themselves.

Darling-Hammond (1998) states that teachers must understand the subject matter fully and be flexible in the approach of this subject matter in order to attempt to address the different learning styles of the students present in a given class. Further Darling-Hammond believes that one way to accomplish this task is to be able to clearly present many concepts and the connections between these concepts. She states that a skillful teacher can use the student interaction with concepts to get them into understanding new ideas.

Helping our students understand themselves holistically is important, but it is only the first step for those interested in helping their students learn. The next step is to synthesize teaching strategies to include all learners.

A Synthesis Approach to Teaching: Auditory, Visual, Tactile

It is most critical to remember that when teaching with individual learning styles in mind, it is rare for any specific class of students to be composed of a group of visual learners, a group of auditory learners, and a group of tactile learners. Our classes tend to have students who possess some characteristics of one, two, or all three of these basic learning styles. Either the students have these characteristics naturally or they have learned throughout their years in education to cope with learning situations and strategies inconsistent with their natural styles.

It is therefore important that we acknowledge not only the innate learning styles of our students, but also the learning strategies that they may have developed. As instructor and student identify both learning styles, the innate and the acquired, the instructor can develop strategies that will better help the student learn. Darling-Hammond (1998) states that and important way to understand and plan for students learning appropriately is to study how students approach the learning process, and the student work that is produced. This information will inform instructors as to student learning style tendencies. As Tomlinson (1999) believes to be effective, a teacher needs to constantly identify where the students are and move them forward from there. This approach is only effective with complete student engagement. Student engagement and motivation to learn is critical for student learning success. If students are comfortable with the type of interaction with learning then they will be motivated, and in turn achieve learning success. Tomlinson (1999) further states that it is important not only to learn facts and data, but also to understand this data conceptually. She states that relying on a fact-driven curriculum will automatically eliminate students with certain learning styles, such as the students who learn holistically with a combination of auditory, visual, and tactile approaches.

Example of Holistic Lessons

Because it is most likely that visual, auditory, and tactile learning styles will all be represented in a given class of students, it is necessary to plan activities to address all three styles at the same time, as much as possible in a holistic way. The holistic approach would have components of lessons/activities that have the auditory, visual, and tactile approaches in mind. This may seem difficult, but it is feasible.

Accommodating each learning style in each lesson does not mean that an entire lesson must be designed covering one concept or one topic in a way that meets the needs of visual, auditory, and tactile learners. What it means is combining techniques in order to address the various learning styles. This may take a little more planning at first, but once an instructor becomes accustomed to thinking in terms of individual learning styles, it becomes easier.

Take, for example, a lesson involving a specific period in history or in literature. An initial introduction of the time period could be done orally, through a lecture about facts that are critical for understanding the period. This introduction would be just that: an introduction. To address the needs of students who are not auditory learners, it is necessary to branch out from the lecture. Another component of the lesson could include such materials as maps, diagrams, artifacts, and documents that represent the period being discussed. These materials naturally help the visual learners understand the period holistically. Allowing the students to interact in a physical manner with these materials will give the tactile learners an opportunity to get involved physically with the period.

Remember, it is not necessary to limit tactile learners to the tactile, visual learners to the visual, and auditory learners to the auditory. Students will naturally gravitate to parts of the lesson with which they feel most comfortable. However, if lessons are designed holistically, as in this example, all students will experience all parts of the lesson and have the chance to learn through their areas of strength, as well as develop their weaker learning style areas.

Consider another example of a holistic lesson in a philosophy class. Philosophy deals with many "What if ...?" questions. When students attempt to make sense out of the world around them and their own realities, often this requires much auditory processing. Because philosophy classes are often arranged in a discussion format, they tend to favor the students with auditory learning styles. If discussions are to benefit all the students, however, they should be combined with additional teaching techniques to address the visual and tactile learning styles.

In addition to the traditional lecture and discussion for a typical philosophy class, the instructor might encourage the students to illustrate their perceptions of their reality or the specific phenomenon being discussed. Some visual learners and tactile learners will find this an effective way to make sense of the topic at hand. However, still other students may need visual representations of the phenomenon being discussed in order to make sense of it right from the start. The tactile learners may need the visual stimulation, but they will need to expand their interaction with the topic by physically representing it in dramatic format or in pantomime.

It is important to provide these different representations so that each student has the opportunity to make sense of the topic and then, in turn, show the instructor, in a way that makes holistic sense, that he or she has understood. This approach to a topic or a concept requires more planning time and more implementation time, but it will address the learning needs of all the students. They will then all understand the material better and be able to apply it to future situations and to understanding other topics or concepts.

Group Activities

Another way to accommodate learning strengths and needs, as well as help expose students to a variety of learning experiences and encourage them to develop other styles, is through group learning situations.

A group situation can provide an opportunity for students of similar learning styles to work together. Each group might then be assigned a task selected to accommodate that specific style. Conversely, working in groups composed of students with diverse learning styles allows students to observe how their classmates learn and to perhaps practice learning styles with which they are less familiar. The group might then be assigned a problem that could be solved in various ways or a task that could be completed from a variety of perspectives.

Group experiences, whether pairs, triads, or larger structures, can provide numerous learning opportunities for the participants. In planning group activities, we should have specific intentions in mind, in terms of our learning objectives and in terms of the objectives for the group experience and the specific goals and objectives for each student. Because each student will bring learning strengths and learning weaknesses to group activities, the concept competency must be part of the objectives, as well as to experience a variety of learning styles.

Experiential Learning Activities

Experiential learning activities are excellent, of course, for tactile learners. Unfortunately, many instructors believe that such activities benefit only the tactile learners. Experiential activities can be implemented to accommodate the learning styles of auditory and visual learners as well.

For example, in a mathematics course, an instructor can show relationships of numbers in a retail setting, such as profit and loss. An experiential activity that requires students to use number theory and number relationships to plan for profit and loss will benefit tactile learners. To expand this activity to aid visual learners, an instructor can use graphs and charts to illustrate trends of profit and loss; such graphics help visual learners process information about number theory and number relationships. To accommodate the auditory learner, the instructor can implement actual pencil-and-paper calculations of numbers using number theory and number relationships; this type of exercise will accommodate the precise, structured auditory learner. This simple example shows how an instructor can address the learning needs of auditory, visual, and tactile learners and promote a successful learning experience for all students.

Interactive Presentations

Interactive presentations can be used in a variety of college courses. They can be implemented in English or history courses, as previously mentioned, and in sociology, psychology, philosophy, or career-oriented courses, as shown in the following examples.

Sociology

An instructor teaching the concept of microsystems could address the needs of all three types of learners through activities that form a cohesive unit of several classes.

To introduce this concept, which includes information about people, roles, and activities in each individual group in a person's life, the instructor could begin with a lecture about what microsystems are, presenting individual facts about microsystems that would eventually lead to the concept as a whole. This type of strategy would address the learning needs of the auditory learner.

Following the introductory lecture, the instructor could implement an activity that might include a web diagram of a variety of typical microsystems that might be present in a person's life. This web diagram could also include a connection component, in which the students represent relationships and similarities among those microsystems. This would give the students the opportunity to evaluate information and synthesize data, using higher-order cognitive skills. This component of the learning strategy would address the needs of the visual learner, who would benefit from having a visual representation of the concept as a whole and being able to identify the individual parts of the whole concept.

To address the tactile learner, the instructor could include a role-playing exercise, with students playing specific roles in one or more of the microsystems. Through such a role-playing exercise, tactile students would have the chance to actually do the concept. Also, the role-playing exercise would provide an additional opportunity for visual learners to see the concept and for auditory learners to hear the concept.

Psychology

In teaching about behaviorism, an instructor might plan activities that focus on the strengths of the three styles. The instructor could plan a simulation that would include the chance for students in the class to interact with other students or organizations on the campus in order to bring about some type of change by implementing certain behaviors. As the students engaged in the simulation, they would be receiving reactions from their target group. The subsequent behaviors would be based upon these reactions. Eventually, with the instructor facilitating, the desired outcome would be reached, through the concept of reward and consequence, positive feedback, and negative feedback.

This simulation would engage the tactile learner in actually doing the concept and the visual learner in actually seeing the concept in reality. However, in order to address the auditory learner, the instructor should take the time at the conclusion of the simulation to outline the specific points of the simulation that exhibit the behaviorist theory. This component of the lesson is important; otherwise, the auditory learner will not comprehend the important pieces of the concept being taught and thus will not understand the concept as a whole.

Philosophy

The concept of a supreme being could be taught with the three learning styles in mind. This type of concept is difficult to present in a multi-faceted way; however, with careful planning it can be done.

Visual and tactile learners can make a model of their interpretation of a supreme being. To accompany this, these learners need to be able to justify what they have created in a holistic description. This strategy addresses the hands-on, creative, and imaginative aspects of visual and tactile learners. Auditory learners could be required to prepare an oral presentation of the characteristics that might be associated with a supreme being. The instructor as facilitator should synthesize the learning situation to include the connection of a supreme being to everyday life, relationships, and whatever general influence it might have. This would enable all learners to comprehend various specific information about the concept as well as comprehend the concept as a whole and its possible lasting effects on life in general.

Career-Oriented Courses

It tends to be easier to organize multifaceted lessons in disciplines that are career oriented. Career-oriented courses often have a practical aspect to their training, such as internships or practica. These types of experiences address the learning needs of tactile and visual learners. However, it is critically important that the course address the needs of auditory learners as well.

Recall that auditory learners need to comprehend the individual pieces of a new concept or process before they truly understand it fully. This means that plunging such learners into a practicum or internship experience before ensuring that they have a preliminary understanding of all that is involved will frustrate them, and they are likely to be unsuccessful in the experience. Therefore, it is critical that instructors of career-oriented courses realize that it is necessary to provide step-by-step information surrounding the concepts involved in order for students to have successful internship or practicum experiences. Also, auditory learners need to understand each concept fully before they can attempt to make connections to the real world through an internship or practicum.

Implications for Teaching and Learning

Learning styles research has many implications for postsecondary instructors. First, we should seriously consider the phenomenon of learning styles: people learn in different ways and sometimes the differences are surprising. Second, teachers at all levels, but especially those at the postsecondary level, because of the traditional reliance on lectures, must look carefully at the information and skills that students are to acquire. This is important because many students who have the ability to learn are being hindered by teaching strategies and techniques that are not compatible with their learning styles.

But how can instructors approach this enormous task?

The first step is to read as much as possible about research on learning styles, to get an overview. Unfortunately, the research reports are sometimes sketchy, they tend to be rather scientific, and they rarely give concrete examples of how to translate the research into practice. Among the most helpful and accessible articles and books are the following (bibliographical information in References):

Butler, Kathleen. *Learning and teaching style: In theory and practice.*

Claxton, Charles S., and Patricia H. Murrell. *Learning styles: Implications for improving educational practices.*

Dunn, Rita, and Kenneth Dunn. *Teaching students through their individual learning styles: A practical approach.*

Grasha, Anthony F., and Laurie Richlin. *Teaching with style.*

Gregorc, Anthony F. *An adult's guide to style.*

Knowles, Malcolm S., and colleagues. *Andragogy in action: Applying modern principles to adult learning.*

Rainey, Mary Ann, and David A. Kolb. *Using experiential learning, theory and learning styles in diversity education.*

Schmeck, Ronald R., ed. *Learning strategies and learning styles.*

Stouch, Catherine A. *What instructors need to know about learning how to learn.*

Reading about research is just the first step. The next step is to act. Unfortunately, there are few specific plans of action. Faculties must organize as groups and administrators must designate professional development time for developing a plan of action.

This plan should consist of a few basic phases. The foundation should be familiarization with research on learning styles, as we have recommended.

Informal Discussion

The next step is for instructors to share what they know about learning styles and how it can be applied. Faculty should organize informal discussion or focus groups so that colleagues can share what they have read about learning styles and, more importantly, how they have interpreted the research. Such discussions would provide participants the chance to better understand the research and gain additional perspectives.

At the end of the time designated for discussion, the group should determine which approach to learning styles it is going to concentrate on. As we have tried to show in this book, there are various approaches and labels used in research, but all the labels have commonalities. Focus groups should highlight specific labels for further work and attempt to integrate related labels.

Analysis of Common Student Behaviors

The next step in implementing learning styles research is to specify student behaviors that illustrate the learning styles targeted for accommodation. Common student behaviors within a classroom setting need to be described, then paired with the designated labels in order to better understand how behaviors reveal learning needs.

Development of Teaching Strategies

Whatever approach to learning styles may be chosen, strategies to accommodate the learning styles need to be deliberate to be most effective and multifaceted—to address more than one style at the same time.

Assume, for example, that the approach is the system used in this book auditory, visual, and tactile. A simplistic illustration of a multifaceted teaching strategy would be to supplement a traditional lecture with visual cues, to address auditory and visual learning styles. It is more difficult to include the tactile learning style. However, when planning lessons or activities becomes deliberate, that is, aimed at addressing all learning styles, the tactile learning style can be included in the overall strategy for individual lessons or complete units of material, through components that involve physical interaction with new material or the movement of students within the classroom or group setting.

Implementation of Teaching Strategies

The process for implementing the teaching strategies that have been developed is threefold. First, we must understand our students and their learning needs. Second, we must take the time to know and understand learning styles research and apply the specific strategies that are appropriate for our students and their situation. Last, we must be committed to continually plan with individual learning styles in mind and to continually use strategies that address the learning styles of our students, modifying those strategies as individual learning needs change.

Assessment

It is not enough to understand learning styles research and to teach according to student styles. Appropriate teaching should always be accompanied by continual assessment. This assessment should cover three areas: learning outcomes, teaching strategies, and student needs.

We should assess what our students have learned and how well they can apply their learning to real world situations or to new concepts that they must learn. Like the teaching strategies, the means of assessment should accommodate the students' learning styles.

We should assess how effective our strategies have been for all of our students. This assessment is related, of course, to the assessment of outcomes. We should then use the results of this assessment to modify the less effective strategies.

We should assess the needs of our students. This process begins with the initial determination of their learning styles and continues until the end of the course. This part of the assessment process must take place throughout any learning experience in order to best ensure continual success. As other student needs are identified, and/or as student needs change, we should modify our teaching strategies.

Implications for Future Teaching and Learning

Learning styles research has given postsecondary instructors the opportunity to ensure learning success for each and every student, each and every semester. This information, summarized and synthesized here allows us to truly understand our students as individual learners with unique learning needs.

It is crucial that instructors understand learning styles research and that they apply what has been discovered. For too long, too many instructors in too many courses have used traditional modes of teaching with too many students. The result: education that benefits primarily students with certain learning styles while disadvantaging students with other styles. This traditional approach in higher education must not continue.

The need is critical for professional development for postsecondary instructors in the area of learning styles. The focus of professional development should be involvement in understanding learning styles research. Further, professional development should include active participation in planning for implementation of learning styles research. This active planning should include curriculum design as well as lesson planning. If curricula are modified to require specific experiences, as well as mastery of certain material, this will promote the infusion of learning styles research into courses and specific lessons.

Understanding and implementing learning styles research is not easy. It requires a commitment on the part of both administrators and instructors, a commitment to learning about the research and a commitment to ensuring that the findings are put into practice. That takes time, funding, and determination.

The most promising hope for further developments in the field of learning styles comes through the commitment of instructors to designing curricula and lessons with learning styles in mind. New information about learning styles and teaching strategies appropriate to them will come from instructors who teach to accommodate their students learning styles. We will all learn more from these experiences and further improve our ways of helping our students learn. The ultimate goal always is the learning success of each and every student.

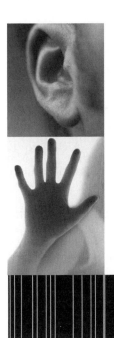

References

Anderson, James A. 1995. Toward a framework for matching teaching and learning styles for diverse populations. In *The importance of learning styles: Understanding the implications for learning, course design, and education,* edited by Ronald R. Sims and Serbrenia J. Sims. Westport CT: Greenwood Press.

Bloom, Benjamin S. 1956. *Taxonomy of educational objectives: The classification of educational goals. Handbook I: Cognitive domain.* New York: Longman.

Butler, Kathleen A. 1988. *Learning and teaching style: In theory and practice.* Revised ed. Columbia CT: Learner's Dimension.

Cahn, Steven M., ed. 1978. *Scholars who teach: The art of college teaching.* Chicago: Nelson-Hall.

Campbell, Linda, Bruce Campbell, and Dee Dickinson. 1996. *Teaching and learning through multiple intelligences*. Needham Heights MA: Allyn & Bacon.

Claxton, Charles S., and Patricia H. Murrell. 1987. *Learning styles: Implications for improving educational practices*. ASHE-ERIC Higher Education Reports, No. 4. Washington DC: Association for the Study of Higher Education.

Darling-Hammond, Linda. 1998. Teacher learning that supports student learning. *Educational Leadership*, 55(5): 6–11.

Dewar, Tammy. 1995. *Adult Learning Online*. www.calliopelearning.com/resources/adult.html

Dunn, Rita. 1990. Rita Dunn answers questions on learning styles. *Educational Leadership*, 48(2): 15–19.

Fahey, John A. 2000. Who wants to differentiate instruction? We did. *Educational Leadership*, 58(1): 70–72.

Felder, R.M. 1996. Matters of style. *ASSE Prism*, 6(4): 18–23.

Feuer, Dale, and Beverly Geber. 1988. Uh-oh … Second thoughts about adult learning theory. *Training*, 25(12): 31–39.

Gardner, Howard. 1983. *Frames of mind: The theory of multiple intelligences*. New York: Basic Books.

Grasha, Anthony F., and Laurie Richlin. 1996. *Teaching with style: A practical guide to enhancing learning by understanding teaching and learning styles*. Pittsburgh PA: Alliance Publishers.

Gregorc, Anthony F. 1985. *An adult's guide to style*. 2nd ed. Columbia CT: Gregorc Associates, Inc.

Gremli, J. 1996. *Knowledge of students characteristics: Definition and checklist*. www.intime.uni/edu/model/teacher/teac1.html

Guild, Pat Burke, and Stephen Garger. 1985. *Marching to different drummers*. Alexandria VA: Association for Supervision and Curriculum Development.

Hand, Katherine L. 1990. Style is a tool for students, too! *Educational Leadership*, 48(2): 13–15.

Harb, John N., S. Olani Durrant, and Ronald E. Terry. 1993. Use of Kolb learning cycle and the 4MAT system in engineering education. *Journal of Engineering Education*, 82(2): 70–77.

Hartman, Virginia F. 1995. Teaching and learning style preferences: Transitions through technology. *VCCA Journal*, 9(2): 18–20.

Hickcox, Leslie K. 1995. Learning styles: A survey of adult learning inventory models. In *The importance of learning styles: Understanding the implications for learning, course design, and education,* edited by Ronald R. Sims and Serbrenia J. Sims. Westport CT: Greenwood Press.

Holloway, John H. 2000. Research links: Preparing teachers for differentiated instruction. *Educational Leadership*, 58(1): 82–84.

Hunter, Walter E., and Louise S. McCants. 1977. The new generation gap: Involvement vs. instant involvement vs. instant information. Topical paper No. 64. ERIC Document Service No. ED 148412. Washington DC: ASHE-ERIC.

Ivey, Gay. 2000. Redesigning reading instruction. *Educational Leadership*, 58(1): 42–45.

Keefe, James W., and John M. Jenkins. 2002. Personalized instruction. *Phi Delta Kappan*, 83(6): 440–448.

Keefe, James W., and Scott D. Thompson. 1987. *Learning style theory and practice.* Reston VA: National Association of Secondary School Principals.

Kelley, Lynn S. 1990. Using 4MAT to improve development, curriculum, and planning. *Educational Leadership,* 48(2): 38–40.

Kelly, Curtis. 1997. *Kolb, David: The theory of experiential learning and ESL.* http://iteslj.org/Articles/Kelly-Experiential/

Knowles, Malcolm S. 1988. *The modern practice of adult education: From pedagogy to andragogy.* Revised and updated. Englewood Cliffs NJ: Cambridge Books.

Knowles, Malcolm S., and Associates. 1984. *Andragogy in action: Applying modern principles to adult learning.* San Francisco: Jossey-Bass.

Kolb, David A. 1984. *Experiential learning: Experience as the source of learning and development.* Englewood Cliffs NJ: Prentice-Hall.

McCarthy, Bernice, et al. 1987. *The 4MAT workbook: Guided practice in 4MAT lesson and unit planning.* New York: EXCEL.

McCarthy, Bernice. 1990. Using the 4MAT system to bring learning styles to schools. *Educational Leadership,* 48(2): 31–36.

Martin, Dianne, and Potter, Les. 1998. How teachers can help students get their learning styles met at school and at home. *Education Summer,* 118(4): 549.

Ojure, Lenna, and Tom Sherman. 2001. Learning styles: Why teachers love a concept research has yet to embrace. *Education Week,* 21(13): 33.

O'Neil, John. 1990. Making sense of style. *Educational Leadership,* 48(2): 4–6.

Pettig, Kim L. 2000. On the road to differentiated practice. *Educational Leadership,* September: 14–18.

Purkiss, William. 1994. Learning styles and their relationship to academic success: A community college perspective. Doctoral dissertation, The Claremont Graduate School.

Rainey, Mary Ann, and David A. Kolb. 1995. Using experiential learning, theory and learning styles in diversity education. In *The importance of learning styles: Understanding the implications for learning, course design, and education,* edited by Ronald R. Sims and Serbrenia J. Sims. Westport CT: Greenwood Press.

Rogers, Spence. 1999. *Teaching tips: 105 Ways to increase motivation and learning.* Nevada City: Performance Learning Systems.

Sagor, Richard. 2003. *Motivating students and teachers in an era of standards.* Alexandria, VA: Association for Supervision and Curriculum Development.

Schmeck, Ronald R., ed. 1988. *Learning strategies and learning styles.* New York: Plenum Press.

Schroeder, Charles C. 1993. www.virtualschool.edu/mon/Academia/KiersyLearningStyles.html

Sealey, Jean. 1985. Instructional strategies. R&D Interpretation Service Bulletin. Available through http://eric.ed.gov.

Sheal, Peter B. 1989. *How to develop and present staff training courses.* London: Kogen Page.

Sims, Ronald R., and Serbrenia J. Sims. 1995a. Learning and learning styles: A review and look at the future. In *The importance of learning styles: Understanding the implications for learning, course design, and education,* edited by Ronald R. Sims and Serbrenia J. Sims. Westport CT: Greenwood Press.

Sims, Ronald R., and Serbrenia J. Sims. 1995b. Learning enhancement in higher education. In *The importance of learning styles: Understanding the implications for learning, course design, and education,* edited by Ronald R. Sims and Serbrenia J. Sims. Westport CT: Greenwood Press.

Sims, Ronald R., and Serbrenia J. Sims, eds. 1995c. *The importance of learning styles: Understanding the implications for learning, course design, and education.* Westport CT: Greenwood Press.

Sims, Serbrenia J. 1995. Experiential learning: Preparing students to move from the classroom to the work environment. In *The importance of learning styles: Understanding the implications for learning, course design, and education,* edited by Ronald R. Sims and Serbrenia J. Sims. Westport CT: Greenwood Press.

Stouch, Catherine A. 1993. What instructors need to know about learning how to learn. In *Applying cognitive learning theory to adult learning,* edited by Daniele D. Flannery. No. 59 (Fall). San Francisco: Jossey-Bass.

Tomlinson, Carol Ann. 1999. Mapping a route toward differentiated instruction. *Educational Leadership,* 57(1): 12–16.

Voss, Margaret A. 1993. I just watched. *Language Arts,* 70(8): 632–663.

Wehrmann, Kari Sue. 2000. Baby steps: A beginner's guide. *Educational Leadership,* 58(1): 20–23.

Wolfe, Particia. 2001. *Brain Matters: Translating research into classroom.* Alexandria, VA, ASCD

Wooldridge, Blue. 1988. Increasing productivity of public sector training. *Public Productivity Review,* 12(2): 205–217.

Zemke, Ron, and Susan Zemke. 1995. Adult learning: What do we know for sure? *Training*, 32(6): 31–40.

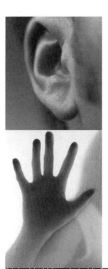

Index

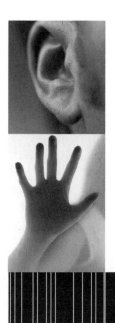

About the Author

L ynne Celli Sarasin is the Deputy Superintendent for Curriculum, Instruction, and Professional Development for Lexington Public Schools in Lexington, MA. She holds a PhD in Curriculum and Instruction from Boston College. She frequently presents workshops and conducts seminars on learning styles. It has also been a primary focus of her professional research and is an outgrowth of her own desire to understand and facilitate the wide range of individual differences she has experienced in her students.